First Workshop on Interactive Learning for Natural Language Processing (InterNLP 2021)

Held online due to COVID-19

AA007976

Bangkok, Thailand
5 August 2021

ISBN: 978-1-7138-3376-5

Printed from e-media with permission by:

Curran Associates, Inc.
57 Morehouse Lane
Red Hook, NY 12571

Some format issues inherent in the e-media version may also appear in this print version.

Copyright© (2021) by the Association for Computational Linguistics and the Asian Federation of Natural Language Processing
All rights reserved.

Printed with permission by Curran Associates, Inc. (2021)

For permission requests, please contact the Association for Computational Linguistics at the address below.

Association for Computational Linguistics
209 N. Eighth Street
Stroudsburg, Pennsylvania 18360

Phone: 1-570-476-8006
Fax: 1-570-476-0860

acl@aclweb.org

Additional copies of this publication are available from:

Curran Associates, Inc.
57 Morehouse Lane
Red Hook, NY 12571 USA
Phone: 845-758-0400
Fax: 845-758-2633
Email: curran@proceedings.com
Web: www.proceedings.com

InterNLP 2021

First Workshop on Interactive Learning for Natural Language Processing

Proceedings of the Workshop

August 5, 2021
Bangkok, Thailand (online)

©2021 The Association for Computational Linguistics
and The Asian Federation of Natural Language Processing

Message from the General Chair

Motivation: A key aspect of human learning is the ability to learn continuously from various sources of feedback. In contrast, much of the recent success of deep learning for NLP relies on large datasets and extensive compute resources to train and fine-tune models, which then remain fixed. This leaves a research gap for systems that adapt to the changing needs of individual users or allow users to continually correct errors as they emerge. Learning from user interaction is crucial for tasks that require a high grade of personalization and for rapidly changing or complex, multi-step tasks where collecting and annotating large datasets is not feasible, but an informed user can provide guidance.
What is interactive NLP?: Interactive Learning for NLP means training, fine-tuning or otherwise adapting an NLP model to inputs from a human user or teacher. Relevant approaches range from active learning with a human in the loop, to training with implicit user feedback (e.g. clicks), dialogue systems that adapt to user utterances and training with new forms of human input. Interactive learning is the converse of learning from datasets collected offline with no human input during the training process.
Goals: The goal of this workshop was to bring together researchers to:

- Develop novel methods for interactive machine learning of NLP models.
- Discuss how to evaluate interactive NLP systems, including models for realistic user simulation.
- Identify scenarios involving natural language where interactive learning is beneficial.

Previous work has been split across different tracks and task-focused workshops, making it hard to disentangle applications from broadly-applicable methodologies or establish common practices for evaluating interactive learning systems. We aimed to bring together researchers to share insights on interactive learning from a wide range of NLP-related fields, including, but not limited to, dialogue systems, question answering, summarization, and educational applications.
Concerning methodology, we encouraged submissions investigating various dimensions of interactive learning, such as (but not restricted to):

- Interactive machine learning methods: the wide range of topics discussed above, from active learning with a user to methods that extract, interpret and aggregate user feedback or preferences from complex interactions, such as natural language instructions.
- User effort: the amount of user effort required for different types of feedback; explicit labels require higher user effort than feedback deduced from user interaction (e.g., clicks, viewtime); how users cope with the system misinterpreting instructions.
- Feedback types: different types of feedback require different techniques to incorporate them into a model. E.g., explicit labels allow us to directly train while user instructions require interpretation.

A major bottleneck for interactive learning approaches is their evaluation, including a lack of suitable datasets. We, therefore, encouraged submissions that cover research into the following:

- Evaluation methods: approaches to assessing interactive methods, such as low-effort, easily reproducible approaches with real-world users and simulated user models for automated evaluation.
- Reproducibility: procedures for documenting user evaluations and ensuring they are reproducible.
- Data: Introduce novel datasets for training and evaluating interactive models.

To investigate scenarios where interactive learning is effective, we invited submissions that present empirical results for applications of interactive methods.

Organizing Committee

- Kianté Brantley (kdbrant@cs.umd.edu) is a fourth year PhD student in Computer Science at The University of Maryland College Park advised by Hal Daumé III. His research interest is in designing algorithms that efficiently integrate domain knowledge into sequential decision-making problems (e.g. reinforcement learning, imitation learning and structure prediction for natural language processing).
- Soham Dan (sohamdan@seas.upenn.edu) is a PhD student at the University of Pennsylvania working with Dan Roth on natural language understanding- specifically, in the context of grounded domains. His research involves concept learning, interactive learning and semantic parsing of instructions.
- Iryna Gurevych (gurevych@ukp.informatik.tu-darmstadt.de) is a full professor in the department of Computer Science at the Technical University of Darmstadt. She has published on interactive methods for NLP in various NLP domains such as language learning, text summarization, or entity linking.
- Ji-Ung Lee (lee@ukp.informatik.tu-darmstadt.de) is a PhD student at the Technical University of Darmstadt. His research focuses on effective model training from user feedback in low-data scenarios coupled with providing the user with instances that fit their needs.
- Filip Radlinski (filiprad@google.com) is a Research Scientist at Google, UK. His research focuses on improvements to conversational search and recommendation through better understanding and modeling user interests through natural language, improved transparency of conversational systems, as well as human-centered evaluation and personalization of information retrieval and recommendation tasks. He received his PhD from Cornell University.
- Hinrich Schütze (hinrichacl@cis.lmu.de) is a full professor at Ludwig Maximilian University, Munich and chair of computational linguistics. His research covers deep learning for NLP, semantics in NLP and linguistics, and information retrieval. He has co-organized several workshops, including two SCLeM workshops (Subword and Character level models in NLP) at EMNLP and NAACL and a Dagstuhl seminar entitled "From Characters to Understanding Natural Language".
- Edwin Simpson (edwin.simpson@bristol.ac.uk) is a lecturer at the University of Bristol working on interactive learning for NLP and machine learning for crowdsourced annotation with an interest in Bayesian methods for handling uncertainty.
- Lili Yu (liliyu@fb.com) is a research scientist in the Facebook Language Research team. Her research interest lies in summarization, conversational AI, learning from user feedback and knowledge representation and grounding.

Table of Contents

Conference Program

August 5th, 2021

Session 1

19:00–19:05 **Opening Remarks**

19:05–19:50 *Invited talk 1*
Dan Goldwasser

19:50–20:20 ***Poster short talks 1***

HILDIF: Interactive Debugging of NLI Models Using Influence Functions
Hugo Zylberajch, Piyawat Lertvittayakumjorn and Francesca Toni

Apple Core-dination: Linguistic Feedback and Learning in a Speech-to-Action Shared World Game
Susann Boy, AriaRay Brown and Morgan Wixted

SHAPELURN: An Interactive Language Learning Game with Logical Inference
Katharina Stein, Leonie Harter and Luisa Geiger

A Proposal: Interactively Learning to Summarise Timelines by Reinforcement Learning
Yuxuan Ye and Edwin Simpson

20:20–21:30 ***Poster session 1***

21:30–22:15 *Invited talk 2 : Beyond Imitation Learning: New Paradigms of Querying and Integrating Different Types of Human Data for Improved Robot Learning*
Dorsa Sadigh

August 5th, 2021 (continued)

Session 2

23:00–23:05 **Opening Remarks**

23:05–23:50 *Invited talk 3 : Continual Language Learning through Collaborative Interaction with Users*
Yoav Artzi

August 6th, 2021

00:00–00:45 *Panel discussion 1*
Julia Kreutzer, Alison Smith-Renner, Ido Dagan

01:00–01:30 ***Poster short talks 2***

Dynamic Facet Selection by Maximizing Graded Relevance
Michael Glass, Md Faisal Mahbub Chowdhury, Yu Deng, Ruchi Mahindru, Nicolas Rodolfo Fauceglia, Alfio Gliozzo and Nandana Mihindukulasooriya

Interactive learning from activity description
Khanh Nguyen, Dipendra Misra, Robert Schapire, Miro Dudík and Patrick Shafto

Active Curriculum Learning
Borna Jafarpour, Dawn Sepehr and Nick Pogrebnyakov

Tackling Fake News Detection by Interactively Learning Representations using Graph Neural Networks
Nikhil Mehta and Dan Goldwasser

01:30–02:45 ***Poster session 2***

03:00–03:45 *Invited talk 4*
Percy Liang

August 6th, 2021 (continued)

Session 3

06:00–06:05 Opening Remarks

06:05–06:50 *Invited talk 5*
Dan Roth

07:00–07:45 *Panel discussion 2*
Seung-won Hwang, Yu Zhou, Dilek Hakkani-Tur

HILDIF: Interactive Debugging of NLI Models Using Influence Functions

Hugo Zylberajch, Piyawat Lertvittayakumjorn, Francesca Toni
Department of Computing, Imperial College London, UK
{hz1820, pl1515, ft}@imperial.ac.uk

Abstract

Biases and artifacts in training data can cause unwelcome behavior in text classifiers (such as shallow pattern matching), leading to lack of generalizability. One solution to this problem is to include users in the loop and leverage their feedback to improve models. We propose a novel explanatory debugging pipeline called **HILDIF**, enabling humans to improve deep text classifiers using influence functions as an explanation method. We experiment on the Natural Language Inference (NLI) task, showing that HILDIF can effectively alleviate artifact problems in fine-tuned BERT models and result in increased model generalizability.

1 Introduction

Given two sentences, a premise and a hypothesis, Natural Language Inference (NLI) is the task of determining whether the premise entails the hypothesis, and it has been considered by many as a sign of language understanding (Condoravdi et al., 2003; Dagan et al., 2005). Although recent deep learning models have shown to achieve good performances on different NLI datasets, as in other tasks, they have been shown to learn shallow heuristics. For example, a model is very likely to predict *entailment* for all hypotheses constructed from words in the premise (McCoy et al., 2019). A key challenge is therefore to understand when and why state-of-the-art NLI models fail and try to mitigate the problems accordingly.

In order to bring to light this kind of pathology, one can use explanation techniques to comprehend how a black box model makes particular predictions. For instance, feature attribution methods explain by identifying parts of inputs that mainly contribute to predictions (Smilkov et al., 2017; Sundararajan et al., 2016; Ribeiro et al., 2016; Lundberg and Lee, 2017). Further, example-based methods, such as influence functions (Koh and Liang, 2017), identify training data points which are the most important for particular predictions. Existing works have proposed ways to improve models by incorporating human feedback, in response to the explanations, by: adding model constraints by fixing certain parameters (Stumpf et al., 2009; Lertvittayakumjorn et al., 2020), adding training samples (Teso and Kersting, 2019), and adjusting models' weights directly (Kulesza et al., 2015).

In this paper, we propose a novel interactive model debugging pipeline called **HILDIF** – **H**uman **I**n the **L**oop **D**ebugging using **I**nfluence **F**unctions. With the NLI task as a target, we use influence functions as an explanation method to help users understand the model reasoning via influential training examples. Then, for each influential example shown, the users provide feedback to create augmented training samples for fine tuning the model. Using HILDIF, we effectively mitigate artifact issues of BERT models (Devlin et al., 2019) trained on the MNLI dataset (Williams et al., 2018) and tested on the HANS dataset (McCoy et al., 2019), which is a known pathological setting for most deep NLI models working on English language. Our code can be found at `https://github.com/hugozylberajch/HILDIF`.

2 Related Work

Influence Functions. Introduced by Hampel (1974), influence functions compute how upweighting individual examples in the training loss changes the model parameters. Influential training examples can also be used to study models (Koh and Liang, 2017). They are particularly useful when feature attribution scores are not sufficient to illustrate how the model *reasons*. In the NLI task, for example, single input words may not suffice to explain a certain prediction, and the overall semantics and structures in the input may be needed.

Proceedings of the First Workshop on Interactive Learning for Natural Language Processing, pages 1–6
August 5, 2021. ©2021 Association for Computational Linguistics

Recently, Han et al. (2020) showed that influence functions can capture key fine-grained interactions among input words and detect the presence of artifacts that lead to incorrect NLI predictions.

Although very appealing, influence functions are computationally expensive. Hence, Koh and Liang (2017) reduced computational complexity by using the **LI**near time **S**tochastic **S**econd order **A**lgorithm (LISSA) for calculating approximations. Guo et al. (2020) proposed FASTIF, which further speeds up the calculation using the k-nearest neighbors algorithm. They also fine tuned the model with influential training samples of *anchor points* (i.e., some data points in the validation set) to correct model errors. We will use FASTIF as a tool to explain BERT model's predictions on the NLI task in our experiment.

Explanatory Interactive Debugging, where we improve a model by leveraging user feedback after presenting explanations for model predictions, was first introduced using simple statistical models such as Naïve Bayes models or Support Vector Machines with simple explanatory techniques (Stumpf et al., 2009). Recently, explanatory debugging has been applied to more complex models using refined interpretability methods. In FIND (Lertvittayakumjorn et al., 2020), a masking matrix is added at the end of a CNN text classifier so as to disable particular CNN filters based on human feedback in response to LRP-based explanations (Arras et al., 2016). In CAIPI (Teso and Kersting, 2019), the user investigates and corrects a LIME-based explanation (Ribeiro et al., 2016) for each prediction. Then additional training samples, created based on the correction, are used to fine tune the model. For more details on explanatory debugging, we refer interested readers to the survey by Lertvittayakumjorn and Toni (2021).

As in CAIPI, we will exploit user feedback to control the generation of augmented samples for fine tuning the model. However, our explanations are influential training samples which are more suitable for explaining NLI predictions. This is an improvement from Guo et al. (2020) that simply fine tuned the model on influential samples without human feedback involved.

3 HILDIF

We propose in Algorithm 1 a new pipeline called **HILDIF** (**H**uman **I**n the **L**oop **D**ebugging with **I**nfluence **F**unctions) for debugging deep text classifiers using influence functions. As far as our knowledge goes, this is the first interactive explanatory debugging algorithm that makes effective use of influence functions. To improve a model f using HILDIF, a set of anchor points $\mathcal{X} = (x_1, x_2, ..., x_n)$ is first selected from the validation dataset $\mathcal{V}$, and the predictions $\hat{\mathcal{Y}} = (\hat{y_1}, \hat{y_2}, ..., \hat{y_n})$ are computed using the model f. Then, for each anchor point x_i, we use FASTIF to identify p influential training samples $\mathcal{Z}_i = (z_{i1}, z_{i2}, ..., z_{ip})$, and we define $\mathcal{Z}$ as a collection of $\mathcal{Z}_i$ for all $x_i \in \mathcal{X}$. Next, for each pair of $(x_i, z_{ij}), i \in \{1, ..., n\}, j \in \{1, ..., p\}$, the user will give a score of similarity s_{ij} that will be used to generate synthetic data using a data augmentation function g. Finally, the model is fine tuned on the new generated data samples.

Algorithm 1: HILDIF. $\mathcal{L}$ is a labeled training set, $\mathcal{V}$ is a labeled validation set, T is the number of iteration, and g is a data augmentation method.

```
t ← 0
f ← FIT(L)
while t < T do
    X ← SELECT_ANCHORS(f, V)
    Ŷ ← f(X)
    Z ← EXPLAIN(f, X, Ŷ)
    S ← Ø
    for x_i ∈ X do
        for z_ij ∈ Z_i do
            Present x_i, ŷ_i, z_ij to the user;
            Obtain a similarity score s_ij for
              the influential example z_ij;
            S ← S ∪ g(z_ij, s_ij)
    f ← FINE_TUNE(f, S)
    t ← t + 1
Return : f
```

Next, we explain, in detail, each step of HILDIF, including explanation generation, user feedback collection, and data augmentation.

Explanation Generation. From the validation set $\mathcal{V}$, we can either select anchor points randomly or handpick some that contain particular heuristics we want to debug. After that, the user is presented with a list of top-p most negatively influential training data points for each anchor point. These influential data points contribute to the decrease of the model's loss when upweighted. Hence, fine-tuning the model using these data points should improve the model performance as studied by Guo et al.

(2020). However, since HILDIF relies on FASTIF which only approximates influence scores, we hypothesize that we can achieve better performance by asking humans to assess relevancy of the influential training samples returned by FASTIF before fine-tuning.

User Feedback Collection. For each anchor point x_i and corresponding influential sample z_{ij}, the user is asked the question: *The test case and the presented sample are: (1) Very different; (2) Different; (3) Can't decide; (4) Similar; (5) Very similar*; the user can then answer by selecting a radio button. Then z_{ij} will obtain a similarity score s_{ij} from 1 to 5 accordingly based on the user's answer. *Similar* in this context means that both samples share the same type of heuristics or lexical artifacts.

Data Augmentation. To create an augmented sample for the NLI task, we have to make sure that the overall semantics of the premise and the hypothesis as well as the overall relation between the two sentences are preserved. We therefore choose random word replacement with synonyms as well as back translation for data augmentation since neither changes the semantic of the sentences. Moreover, we found empirically by testing different configurations that generating $10 \times s_{ij}$ augmented samples for the influential sample z_{ij} yielded the best results. For instance, an influential sample with the score 3 leads to 30 augmented samples with the same label as the original sample.

4 Experimental Setup

Datasets and Models. We evaluate our pipeline with a pretrained BERT-base cased model. We use the MNLI dataset (Williams et al., 2018) for training and validation, and the HANS dataset, which is known to be a dataset where BERT performs poorly (McCoy et al., 2019), for testing. For the MNLI training and validation set, we merge the class *neutral* and *contradiction* into a single *non-entailment* class, following the HANS dataset's setting. HANS targets three heuristics of NLI and includes examples showcasing these heuristics: *Lexical Overlap* where the hypothesis is constructed with words from the premise, *Constituent*, where the hypothesis is a subtree of the premise's parse tree, and *Subsequence*, where the hypothesis is a contiguous subsequence of the premise (see Table 1 in the Appendix for some examples). NLI models almost always predict entailment for any example containing these heuristics although sometimes the correct label is non-entailment. So, our goal is to make the model better detect non-entailment cases while maintaining its performance on the entailment cases. For the overall performance, we chose accuracy as our evaluation metric because HANS is a balanced dataset (containing, for each subgroup of heuristics, 5,000 samples of the entailment class and 5,000 samples of the non-entailment class).

Implementation Details. All our models are implemented using the pytorch library and trained using the AdamW optimizer. The HANS dataset is held-out during training and fine-tuning and is only used for testing. For computing influence functions, we use the FASTIF algorithm and FAISS library (Johnson et al., 2019) for k-nearest neighbors search. Finally, we ran all our experiment on a single 12GB NVIDIA Tesla K80 GPU. With this setting, the computation of influence scores of 5,000 training points for a corresponding anchor point takes approximately seven minutes. The BERT-base model is trained for two epochs on the MNLI training dataset.

Regarding user feedback collection, due to human resources constraints, we did our interactive experiments with one expert user. Further experiments could be conducted with more users, and results for the same pair of anchor point and influential point could be aggregated in order to reduce human bias.

Comparison. We experimented with $T = 1$, using five anchor points with 10 and 20 influential samples each. We introduce three binary propositions that will define the debugging pipeline: HS: Human scoring, DA: Data augmentation, and H: Handpicked anchor points. Without human scoring ($\neg HS$), every influential sample receives a score of 5. Without data augmentation ($\neg DA$), the fine tuning is done on each influential sample only, and without handpicked anchor points ($\neg H$), anchor points are selected randomly. Note that our handpicked anchor points were chosen among the validation samples that contain either the lexical overlap or the subsequence heuristic (see Table 2 in the Appendix). We compared the performance of eight different configurations of debugging algorithms that stem from these three binary propositions. For each configuration, we trained and im-

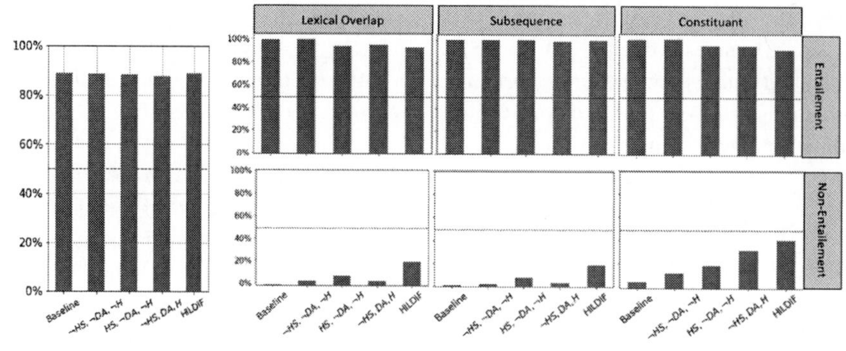

(a) (b)

Configuration			10 influential points			20 influential points		
			LO	SUB	CON	LO	SUB	CON
HS	DA	H	(93.99 , 18.16)	(98.90 , 12.10)	(92.99 , 36.10)	(92.70 , **20.76**)	(99.24 , **18.80**)	(90.82 , **41.58**)
		$\neg H$	(98.89 , 3.56)	(99.66 , 2.74)	(97.12 , 12.10)	(98.12 , 2.06)	(98.51 , 4.20)	(97.22 , 19.21)
	$\neg DA$	H	(95.51 , 6.81)	(96.40 , 5.32)	(93.71 , 22.28)	(98.94 , 8.64)	(97.81 , 3.40)	(95.01 , 19.32)
		$\neg H$	(98.81 , 2.16)	(98.73 , 2.25)	(95.55 , 16.12)	(99.09 , 1.91)	(98.89 , 2.12)	(93.39 , 17.64)
$\neg HS$	DA	H	(99.42 , 2.94)	(99.65 , 3.15)	(96.01 , 32.15)	(99.32 , 3.76)	(99.20 , 4.01)	(94.99 , 32.34)
		$\neg H$	(99.10 , 1.86)	(99.81 , 2.84)	(97.67 , 9.66)	(98.10 , 2.40)	(98.89 , 3.90)	(96.20 , 17.01)
	$\neg DA$	H	(98.13 , 3.10)	(99.62 , 2.87)	(97.03 , 9.99)	(97.21 , 4.01)	(99.68 , 2.61)	(96.54 , 13.13)
		$\neg H$	(99.49 , 0.90)	(99.32 , 1.67)	(97.88 , 6.10)	(99.12 , 1.12)	(99.01 , 1.29)	(97.15 , 5.99)
Baseline			**LO**: (99.56 , 0.98) **SUB**: (100.00 , 1.30) **CON**: (99.02 , 5.74)					

(c)

Figure 1: HS stands for Human Scoring, DA for Data Augmentation and H for Handpicked anchor points. (a) Average accuracy on the MNLI test set (b) Accuracies on the HANS evaluation set, which has 3 heuristic categories and 2 classes. Dashed lines show chance performance. (c) Accuracies on the HANS evaluation set for different configurations of all the debugging procedures. LO stands for Lexical Overlap, SUB for Subsequence, and CON for Constituent category of heuristics. For each cell, the first value of the tuple is the accuracy on the entailment class and the second is the accuracy on the non-entailment class. Best scores for the non-entailment class in bold.

proved three models using different random seeds and averaged the final performance on the test set. Note that the $(\neg HS, \neg DA, \neg H)$ configuration is the algorithm used in Guo et al. (2020) whereas the (HS, DA, H) and $(HS, DA, \neg H)$ configurations are our HILDIF algorithm.

5 Results

Figure 1b shows the accuracies on the HANS dataset of the baseline model (i.e., BERT trained on MNLI), and of four configurations, including (HS, DA, H) which is displayed as HILDIF in the figure. We can see that HILDIF consistently achieved a higher accuracy in all three categories of heuristics for the non-entailment class and a slightly lower accuracy for the entailment class. Actually, we observe the trade-off between the accuracies of both classes in all the four configurations. However, HILDIF still got higher overall accuracy on the HANS dataset than the baseline and the other configurations. Moreover, interactive debugging with human scores yielded better accuracies than debugging without human scores for the Lexical Overlap and the Subsequence categories. Meanwhile, on the Constituent category, handpicking anchor points with targeted heuristic led to a big jump in accuracy that outperformed the configuration with human feedback but random anchor points. Therefore, incorporating human knowledge since the selecting anchors step is also helpful when we have prior knowledge about the model bugs. Note also, in Figure 1a, that the model accuracies on the MNLI for HILDIF and the other configurations stay close to the baseline model's accuracy, as desired.

The table in Figure 1c shows that fine tuning the model with augmented data samples, instead of the influential samples only, gave better results in most cases. This was likely because data augmentation could help prevent the model from overfitting the influential samples. Besides, there was little to no improvement in the model performance when we added user feedback (i.e., human scores) for random anchor points but a substantial improvement for handpicked anchor points. This can be because, during user feedback collection, most of the data samples are difficult to compare as they either satisfy several heuristics or no heuristics relevant to the NLI task. When looking at some influential samples for handpicked anchor points, most satisfy the same heuristic and, if not, they can be easily spotted by human eyes. Although we are still far from chance performance on the non-entailment class, HILDIF achieved a substantial increase in accuracy with just five anchor points.

6 Conclusion

We introduced HILDIF, an interactive explanatory debugging pipeline for deep text classifiers, and ran experiments on the NLI task, achieving high accuracies with MNLI-trained BERT across all categories of the pathological HANS dataset. Future work includes enhancement of the data augmentation part, including the use of a variational autoencoder or a GPT-2 based generative model for synthetic data generation. Also, with more human resources, experiments can be conducted by fine-tuning more than one iterations ($T > 1$) with more anchor points for each iteration. Finally, it would be interesting to apply HILDIF to other text classification tasks, given that, except for the handpicked anchor points that are chosen with knowledge of the task, every step of the pipeline is task-independent.

References

Leila Arras, Franziska Horn, Grégoire Montavon, Klaus-Robert Müller, and Wojciech Samek. 2016. Explaining predictions of non-linear classifiers in NLP. In *Proceedings of the 1st Workshop on Representation Learning for NLP*, pages 1–7, Berlin, Germany. Association for Computational Linguistics.

Cleo Condoravdi, Dick Crouch, Valeria de Paiva, Reinhard Stolle, and Daniel G. Bobrow. 2003. Entailment, intensionality and text understanding. In *Proceedings of the HLT-NAACL 2003 Workshop on Text Meaning*, pages 38–45.

Ido Dagan, Oren Glickman, and Bernardo Magnini. 2005. The pascal recognising textual entailment challenge. In *Proceedings of the PASCAL Challenges Workshop on Recognising Textual Entailment*.

Jacob Devlin, Ming-Wei Chang, Kenton Lee, and Kristina Toutanova. 2019. BERT: Pre-training of deep bidirectional transformers for language understanding. In *Proceedings of the 2019 Conference of the North American Chapter of the Association for Computational Linguistics: Human Language Technologies, Volume 1 (Long and Short Papers)*, pages 4171–4186, Minneapolis, Minnesota. Association for Computational Linguistics.

Han Guo, Nazneen Fatema Rajani, Peter Hase, Mohit Bansal, and Caiming Xiong. 2020. Fastif: Scalable influence functions for efficient model interpretation and debugging. *arXiv preprint arXiv:2012.15781*.

Frank R. Hampel. 1974. The influence curve and its role in robust estimation. *Journal of the American Statistical Association*, 69(346):383–393.

Xiaochuang Han, Byron C. Wallace, and Yulia Tsvetkov. 2020. Explaining black box predictions and unveiling data artifacts through influence functions. In *Proceedings of the 58th Annual Meeting of the Association for Computational Linguistics*, pages 5553–5563, Online. Association for Computational Linguistics.

J. Johnson, M. Douze, and H. Jégou. 2019. Billion-scale similarity search with gpus. *IEEE Transactions on Big Data*, pages 1–1.

Pang Wei Koh and Percy Liang. 2017. Understanding black-box predictions via influence functions. In *Proceedings of the 34th International Conference on Machine Learning*, volume 70 of *Proceedings of Machine Learning Research*, pages 1885–1894. PMLR.

Todd Kulesza, Margaret Burnett, Weng-Keen Wong, and Simone Stumpf. 2015. Principles of explanatory debugging to personalize interactive machine learning. In *Proceedings of the 20th International Conference on Intelligent User Interfaces*, IUI '15, page 126–137, New York, NY, USA. Association for Computing Machinery.

Piyawat Lertvittayakumjorn, Lucia Specia, and Francesca Toni. 2020. FIND: Human-in-the-Loop Debugging Deep Text Classifiers. In *Proceedings of the 2020 Conference on Empirical Methods in Natural Language Processing (EMNLP)*, pages 332–348, Online. Association for Computational Linguistics.

Piyawat Lertvittayakumjorn and Francesca Toni. 2021. Explanation-based human debugging of nlp models: A survey. *arXiv preprint arXiv:2104.15135*.

Scott Lundberg and Su-In Lee. 2017. A unified approach to interpreting model predictions. *arXiv preprint arXiv:1705.07874*.

Tom McCoy, Ellie Pavlick, and Tal Linzen. 2019. Right for the wrong reasons: Diagnosing syntactic heuristics in natural language inference. In *Proceedings of the 57th Annual Meeting of the Association for Computational Linguistics*, pages 3428–3448, Florence, Italy. Association for Computational Linguistics.

Marco Tulio Ribeiro, Sameer Singh, and Carlos Guestrin. 2016. "why should i trust you?" explaining the predictions of any classifier. In *Proceedings of the 22nd ACM SIGKDD international conference on knowledge discovery and data mining*, pages 1135–1144.

Daniel Smilkov, Nikhil Thorat, Been Kim, Fernanda Viégas, and Martin Wattenberg. 2017. Smoothgrad: removing noise by adding noise. *arXiv preprint arXiv:1706.03825*.

Simone Stumpf, Vidya Rajaram, Lida Li, Weng-Keen Wong, Margaret Burnett, Thomas Dietterich, Erin Sullivan, and Jonathan Herlocker. 2009. Interacting meaningfully with machine learning systems: Three experiments. *International journal of human-computer studies*, 67(8):639–662.

Mukund Sundararajan, Ankur Taly, and Qiqi Yan. 2016. Gradients of counterfactuals. *arXiv preprint arXiv:1611.02639*.

Stefano Teso and Kristian Kersting. 2019. Explanatory interactive machine learning. In *Proceedings of the 2019 AAAI/ACM Conference on AI, Ethics, and Society*, AIES '19, page 239–245, New York, NY, USA. Association for Computing Machinery.

Adina Williams, Nikita Nangia, and Samuel Bowman. 2018. A broad-coverage challenge corpus for sentence understanding through inference. In *Proceedings of the 2018 Conference of the North American Chapter of the Association for Computational Linguistics: Human Language Technologies, Volume 1 (Long Papers)*, pages 1112–1122, New Orleans, Louisiana. Association for Computational Linguistics.

A Examples and Anchor Points

Table 1 shows an example from the MNLI dataset (Williams et al., 2018) and three examples from the HANS dataset (each of which has a different heuristic type) (McCoy et al., 2019). Besides, Table 2 shows the five handpicked anchor points used in the experiment.

MNLI Dataset
$\mathcal{P}$: News ' cover says the proliferation of small computer devices and the ascendance of Web-based applications are eroding Microsoft's dominance. $\mathcal{H}$: Microsoft is a more profitable company than Apple. **Label**: non-entailment
HANS Dataset (Lexical Overlap)
$\mathcal{P}$: The professors advised the judge. $\mathcal{H}$: The judge advised the professors. **Label**: non-entailment
HANS Dataset (Subsequence)
$\mathcal{P}$: The professor who introduced the doctors recognized the secretaries. $\mathcal{H}$: The doctors recognized the secretaries. **Label**: non-entailment
HANS Dataset (Constituent)
$\mathcal{P}$: Certainly the senators recognized the actor. $\mathcal{H}$: The senators recognized the actor. **Label**: entailment

Table 1: Examples of premises and hypotheses from the MNLI dataset and the HANS dataset. $\mathcal{P}$ and $\mathcal{H}$ stand for premise and hypothesis, respectively.

$\mathcal{P}$: Similar conclusions have been reached by state legal needs ' studies in a dozen states including Florida , Georgia , Hawaii , Illinois , Indiana , Kentucky , Maryland , Massachusetts , Missouri , Nevada , New York , and Virginia , using a variety of methodologies for estimating the unmet legal needs of the poor. $\mathcal{H}$: Similar conclusions have been reached by state legal needs ' studies. **Label**: entailment **Heuristics**: Subsequence
$\mathcal{P}$: From Cockpit Country to St . Ann ' s Bay. $\mathcal{H}$: From St . Ann ' s Bay to Cockpit Country. **Label**: non-entailment **Heuristics**: Lexical Overlap, Reverse Ordering
$\mathcal{P}$: Shoot only the ones that face us , Jon had told Adrin. $\mathcal{H}$: Shoot the ones that face us , Adrin told Jon. **Label**: non-entailment **Heuristics**: Lexical Overlap, Reverse Ordering
$\mathcal{P}$: Just north of the Shalom Tower is the Yemenite Quarter , its main attractions being the bustling Carmel market and good Oriental restaurants. $\mathcal{H}$: The Shalom Tower is north of the Yemenite Quarter. **Label**: non-entailment **Heuristics**: Lexical Overlap, Reverse Ordering
$\mathcal{P}$: Life , unlike Reich ' s book , is not a series of morality fables. $\mathcal{H}$: Reich ' s book is a series of morality fables. **Label**: entailment **Heuristics**: Lexical Overlap, Negation

Table 2: Five handpicked anchor points from the MNLI validation set, with specific heuristics. $\mathcal{P}$ and $\mathcal{H}$ stand for premise and hypothesis, respectively.

Apple Core-dination: Linguistic Feedback and Learning in a Speech-to-Action Shared World Game

Susann Boy*
Saarland University

AriaRay Brown
Saarland University

Morgan Wixted
Saarland University

{susannb,ariaray,morganw}@coli.uni-saarland.de

Introduction. We investigate the question of how adaptive feedback from a virtual agent impacts the linguistic input of the user in a shared world game environment. To do so, we carry out an exploratory pilot study to observe how individualized linguistic feedback affects the user's instructional speech input. We introduce a speech-controlled game, Apple Core-dination, in which an agent learns complex tasks using a base knowledge of simple actions.

Apple Core-dination is a shared-world language building game that situates the user and agent in a common virtual space. The agent is equipped with a learning mechanism for mapping new commands to sequences of simple actions, as well as the ability to incorporate user input into written responses. To build a framework for mapping new language and actions to existing knowledge, our game adopts concepts from the semantic parsing model of Artzi and Zettlemoyer (2013), which makes use of situated cues and common constructs found in instructional language. We seed the knowledge of the agent by providing an initial lexicon of text-to-action mappings for basic movements and communicative functionalities. The agent repeatedly shares its internal knowledge state by responding to what it knows and does not know about language meaning and the shared environment.

Our paper focuses on the linguistic feedback loop in order to analyze the nature of user input. Feedback from the agent is provided in the form of visual movement and written linguistic responses. Particular attention is given to incorporating user input into agent responses and updating the speech-to-action mappings based on commands provided by the user. Since the portrayal of an agent can affect how the user perceives its emotional intelligence (Chita-Tegmark et al., 2019) and trustworthiness (Fan et al., 2017), we consider visual cues that may also contribute to the user's choice of language when interacting. The focus of building agent knowledge is based on enriching the mappings of linguistic input to sequences of simple actions for a given user session. Our system also gives the user control over the mechanism of speech input by providing multiple key-press activated speech-to-text models. Through our pilot study, we analyze task success and compare the lexical features of user input. Results show variation in input length and lexical variety across users, suggesting a correlation between the two that can be studied further.

Background. Cooperative language building games allow the user and agent to jointly accomplish a shared task through language collaboration. Previous research in cooperative language building games has shown that success can be achieved through accommodation between the user and the agent, where both user and agent adapt their communication to adjust to the communicative needs of the other. The interaction can result in user language becoming "more consistent, less verbose, and more precise" as users adapt to the perceived abilities of the computer (Wang et al., 2016). Accommodation of user language supports findings in human-human interaction in which speakers tend to infer the linguistic and situational awareness of their interlocutors (Pickering and Garrod, 2004). Even low effort from the computer agent to cooperate with the user can lead users to believe common ground is established (Chai et al., 2014). Perceived common ground, or a common understanding of the shared environment, can be achieved through the goal of a shared task along with the agent's effort to make apparent its internal knowledge state.

Speech-to-Action Shared World Game. Apple Core-dination embodies the computer in a person-

* All authors have equal contribution.

Proceedings of the First Workshop on Interactive Learning for Natural Language Processing , pages 7–15
August 5, 2021. ©2021 Association for Computational Linguistics

ified agent that prompts the user to teach it new tasks through learning and cooperative interaction. The agent's internal knowledge of its progress is shared through linguistic and action-based feedback. We use the player's own speech (the input) to customize agent responses (the output). The resulting system allows us to analyze how individualized feedback affects the nature of user input. Game implementation code is available on GitHub[1]

Game Environment. The game begins with an introduction in which the user first learns to interact with the agent by naming it through speech. The goal of the game is to complete a set of tasks framed as **complex actions**. The user teaches the agent to achieve the given tasks through multi-step speech commands that build upon **basic actions** already known by the agent. A mid-session view of the game screen is shown in Figure 1. Additional game views are offered in Appendix A.

Figure 1: The game interface. The tasks are displayed on the right side and at the bottom appears the agent's feedback while executing a command.

The basic actions of the agent can be triggered by uttering corresponding commands. Basic actions include simple movement functions in all four directions (left, right, up, down), general movement (move), object destinations (e.g. tree, bridge, itself), repetition of previous actions, greeting the user, and reacting to positive and negative feedback such as *good job* or *no, not that.*

The agent can store new learned commands into its knowledge base via the `yes` function triggered by the word *yes*. Upon completion of a task, the `yes` function is silently called in order to add the the relevant task instructions to the agent's learned commands. A subsequent utterance of the learned task instruction (e.g. *climb the tree*) will directly access the `climb_tree` function. Although the

[1]https://github.com/ariabee/applecore

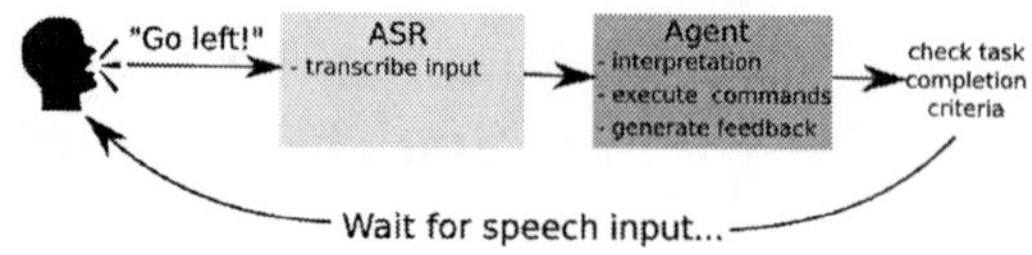

Figure 2: Description of the game loop. The user gives speech input which is transcribed by a speech-to-text model. The transcribed instruction is then interpreted by the agent and feedback is generated. If the instruction is in the agent's knowledge base, an action is executed. The game checks if the action led to the completion of a task and then waits for the next instruction.

agent can move to the location of objects in its knowledge base, it does not contain action functions to interact with the objects. While executing a command, the agent gives a response in the form of text feedback on the screen and movement to a destination when applicable.

Speech-to-Text. Our speech-to-text system provides users with the ability to play our game using their voice. We currently have two systems implemented: Google Cloud Speech API (Zhang, 2017) and SpeechBrain's pre-trained automatic speech recognition (ASR) model (Ravanelli et al., 2021). With both of these models, we can experiment to see the interactions between the users and the ability to choose between different speech recognition systems.

Our speech-to-text pipeline is as follows: our users give speech input by pressing and holding a key (*M* or *SPACE*) that accesses the speech-to-text model. The input is recorded using Python's speech recognition library (Zhang, 2017) and transcribed using the selected model. A single .wav file is saved locally and rewritten for each utterance that uses the SpeechBrain model.

Agent Knowledge and Language Parsing. The agent embodies the language knowledge and learning mechanism of the game. The agent has access to a knowledge base, a **transcript** that serves as long-term memory, interpretation methods for parsing linguistic input, and internal properties that act as working memory. The agent's **knowledge** also contains **hidden actions**, or functions representing the complex game tasks. These functions are hidden in the sense that the agent cannot initially access them through their corresponding instructions. Figure 3 is referenced for explanation.

The knowledge base contains a **lexicon** of known words mapped to action functions, a dictionary of **learned phrases** that fills as the game

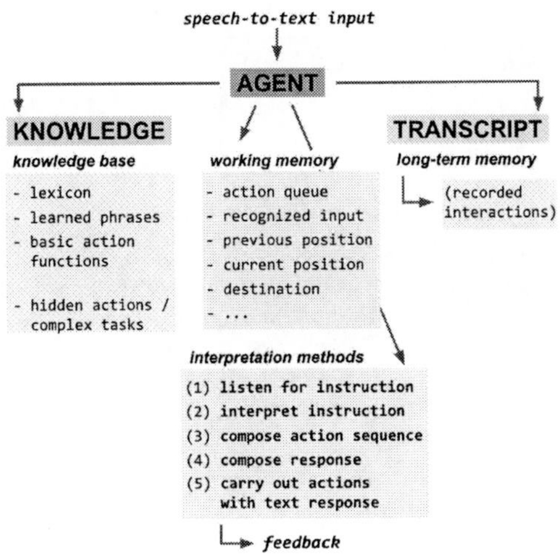

Figure 3: Model of the agent knowledge and language processing mechanism in Apple Core-dination.

progresses, a list of actions mapping indices to action functions, and the individual action functions which represent basic actions. Each piece of language that the agent recognizes is mapped to the related **action functions**. Knowledge also holds the hidden actions that represent the given complex tasks that the agent cannot yet access through mapped language, e.g. the tasks *climb the tree*, *cross the bridge*, and *find red flowers*.

The transcript serves the role of **long-term memory**, in case the agent needs to reference a previous instruction, action sequence, or response. The transcript updates and saves to a structured data file in every game loop. The file contains information about which of the two speech-to-text models was accessed, which instruction the user has given to the agent (output of the speech-to-text model), the response of the agent, and what sequence of actions was executed after the command. We track the progression of the game by storing whether the performed actions led to the completion of a task.

The agent has the ability to map both new and recognized utterances to actions. The function for confirmation and learning links the previous command to a successful sequence of actions performed by the agent. When an instruction is given, the agent parses and composes the utterance into an executable action sequence, or list of indexed action functions. Each function of the event is then executed during the game loop. Successfully completing a task will map the original task command to the hidden task function, adding the phrase-to-action mapping to the agent's learned phrases. Henceforth, input containing the task command will trigger the learned task function.

We implement a simplified parsing mechanism to compose input strings into meaningful combinations of mapped action functions. Parsing involves first searching for learned phrases, followed by checking the remaining string for recognized words that exist in the lexicon. Known words and phrases along with their corresponding actions are stored in the agent's **working memory**. The list of actions is then composed into a list of single actions and combined based on semantic meaning. The completed sequence is stored in an **action queue**. Each action contributes to building the agent's response by returning a string based on the input that triggered the action. Once the response is composed, each action in the queue is executed one at a time in the game loop.

Linguistic Feedback. When a user gives an instruction (e.g. *walk there to the left*), part of the utterance is incorporated into the response of the agent (e.g. *walking somewhere going left*). Feedback from the agent then becomes input for the user, while also informing the user about the nature of the agent's knowledge, or what it does or does not know about language meaning and its surrounding environment.

The nature of individualized feedback is dependent on each basic action function. The part of the utterance that triggered each action is sent as an argument when processing the function for response-only output. Constructed feedback from each mapped utterance is concatenated to form the agent's response. For instructions containing learned phrases, the entire learned string is returned as feedback. For example, the instruction *hop up to the tree* will initially result in the response, *going up going to the tree*. When the phrase is learned, the agent will respond instead with the recognized learned phrase *hop up to the tree* that maps to moving up and to the position of the tree. An example instruction with resulting linguistic feedback is provided in Appendix B.

The agent also provides feedback for fully unrecognized input; e.g. *climb the tall plant* would result in the agent response: *how do I climb the tall plant?*, where the unrecognized phrase is incorporated into agent feedback. Upon learning this new command, the agent would respond: *yes, I learned to climb the tall plant.*

Pilot Study. We tested our game in an exploratory pilot study of five English-speaking volunteers who were only instructed to play the game but not obligated to complete all tasks in the game. Participants were given instructions for using each speech-to-test system, but not directed to use either or both. We evaluate the interaction between agent and user with the agent's long-term memory, the transcript. The transcript files include information about which key they pressed to give an instruction, the instruction transcribed by the speech-to-text model, the actions triggered by the command, the linguistic feedback given by the agent and whether the command led to the completion of a task.

In completed transcripts, the instructions were manually annotated by one of the authors as *clean* if the speech-to-text model correctly transcribed the instruction. Only cleaned instructions were used for analysis, as incorrect model output does not indicate a successful interaction between user and agent. However, if the intended action was triggered even though one or more words were transcribed wrongly, the instruction was still marked as clean. The users were asked to anonymously send us or upload their transcript files. We gathered 219 commands in total, of which 182 were annotated as clean transcriptions.

Our main interest is how the user interacts with the agent. The usage of two speech-to-text models enables us to evaluate their performance based on the preference of the users.

Results. We examine two lexical factors of the instructions: *quantity* and *quality* of the command. Quantity in this context refers to the length of the phrase (how many words were used), and quality is a measure of how large the user's vocabulary is (how many different words were used). Table 1 shows relevant statistics regarding the instructions by each user.

Instruction lengths and vocabulary size were obtained from the cleaned transcripts (only utterances that the speech-to-text model transcribed correctly). We found that the range of the instruction length is quite wide (one to 11 words), but the average instruction length of 3.7 words suggests that users tend to use single short commands. The agent can perform multiple actions, but the players rarely made use of this. This observation is in agreement with studies by Marge et al. (2020). The quality of a user's instructions is defined by their vocabulary size, which was determined by counting the number of unique words uttered by each user. The average vocabulary size is 35.4 words. User 4, who uttered the shortest instructions on average, also has the smallest vocabulary size (20 words), and User 2 has the largest vocabulary (53 words), but their instruction length is below average. Future work will more precisely examine the interaction between quality and quantity of user input and whether it corresponds to agent feedback or individual participant differences.

	User1	User2	User3	User4	User5	average
instruction length (min-max)	1-5	1-7	3-11	1-5	1-11	1.4-7.8
average instruction length	3.1	3.3	5.8	2.3	3.8	3.7
vocab size	28	53	38	20	38	35.4
M key (clean output)	44 (27)	0	0	4 (1)	0	9.6
SPACE bar (clean output)	4 (3)	52 (47)	19 (19)	46 (42)	50 (43)	34.2

Table 1: Relevant interaction data between each user and the agent: Shortest and longest instruction, average instruction length, vocabulary size (number of unique words) and number of times *M* (SpeechBrain) or *SPACE* (Google Speech) was pressed (and how many times the speech was transcribed well).

Task	User1	User2	User3	User4	User5	average
Go to the tree	1	2	2	5	2	2.4
Climb the tree			9		2	5.5
Cross the bridge		10		7	21	12.7
Find red flowers				7	15	11

Table 2: Instructions needed by each user until a task was completed.

The linguistic feedback helped the players to communicate successfully with the agent. They often repeated their previous command when the speech-to-text model did not correctly transcribe their utterance.

Table 2 shows how many instructions the users uttered until a task was completed. The first task (*go to the tree*) can be completed with one command since the agent has it already in its knowledge base. This task acts as positive reinforcement for the user to continue completing tasks and marks a common point across users where utterances become more task-directed. It was also the only task that all users completed: User 1 achieved it after one command, User 4 needed five commands. Only a single player completed all four tasks, which could mean that it is not clear how to complete some of the tasks or that the game is not engaging enough.

We used multiple speech-to-text models to evaluate which model was preferred by our users in terms of user interaction. Table 1 shows that the

SPACE bar was pressed more often than the *M* key, meaning that the Google model was accessed more often. Only User 1 used the *M* key in the majority of speech commands to the agent and three out of the five users did not use the second model at all. This could be due to preferred usability (the *SPACE* bar is easier to press than the *M* key), that one model produces cleaner and faster transcriptions compared to the other model, or simply that users forget there is a second model option.

Transcription accuracy from either model can affect feedback, user-agent interaction, and game progression in several cases of interest. In one example, the Google model transcribed the instruction *go up* as **co-op*, which resulted in the response *how do I co-op?* and no movement from the agent. For User 1 who accessed both models, the SpeechBrain model transcribed the instruction *go left* as *go *lift*, which resulted in the response of *going somewhere*, since the agent recognized only the word *go* from its knowledge base. Both examples exhibit failed instructions from transcription errors, since the input did not lead to successful parsing of the intended actions. However, only the former reveals the incorrect transcription. In the latter case, the user is not notified that *left* was absent from the feedback because it was transcribed as *lift*. In cases of misalignment due to transcription error, the user could attempt to clarify the command, if simple clarification seems possible, or opt for a new speech-to-text model altogether. For future experiments, we will encourage users to try either system to see if they have a preference, especially when it is clear that a command was not properly interpreted.

Future Work. Results from user-agent interactions in the pilot study inform improvements that can be made to the game environment. These include expanding the agent's baseline knowledge, increasing the complexity in agent parsing abilities, and more finely incorporating user input into feedback responses. More grammatically formed feedback for learned phrases could be processed with the addition of a semantic parser. The response for a learned phrase *dance left and slide right* would appear more realistic and sophisticated if it occurred from the agent in the gerund verb form as *dancing left and sliding right*.

We plan to carry out a larger comparative study of user input in Apple Core-dination. Players will be divided into two groups: one where the agent gives individualized linguistic feedback and one where it gives action-only feedback. By providing a clear choice of speech-to-text models, we can better assess the interaction between model accuracy, agent response, and user behavior to determine whether the user's preference for a model becomes a factor in resolving agent understanding.

Our current results show variation in quantity and quality of input across users, which will be investigated further. The user's language adjustment over time may also vary when the agent responses are shown to increasingly accommodate user input. Individualized linguistic feedback should better inform the user of how the agent processes input and adapts to new knowledge from the user. It should also allow users to speak to the agent through preferred utterances, and help them to resolve communication errors when they struggle to complete a task.

Acknowledgments. We would like to thank the anonymous reviewers for their valuable feedback. We also thank our anonymous participants for their help, and Dr. Lucia Donatelli for her insightful comments and suggestions throughout.

References

Yoav Artzi and Luke Zettlemoyer. 2013. Weakly supervised learning of semantic parsers for mapping instructions to actions. *Transactions of the Association for Computational Linguistics*, 1:49–62.

Joyce Y. Chai, Lanbo She, Rui Fang, Spencer Ottarson, Cody Littley, Changsong Liu, and Kenneth Hanson. 2014. Collaborative effort towards common ground in situated human-robot dialogue. HRI '14, page 33–40, New York, NY, USA. Association for Computing Machinery.

M. Chita-Tegmark, M. Lohani, and M. Scheutz. 2019. Gender effects in perceptions of robots and humans with varying emotional intelligence. In *2019 14th ACM/IEEE International Conference on Human-Robot Interaction (HRI)*, pages 230–238.

Lisa Fan, Matthias Scheutz, Monika Lohani, Marissa McCoy, and Charlene Stokes. 2017. Do we need emotionally intelligent articial agents? first results of human perceptions of emotional intelligence in humans compared to robots. In *Proceedings of the Seventeenth International Conference on Intelligent Virtual Agents*.

Matthew Marge, Felix Gervits, Gordon Briggs, Matthias Scheutz, and Antonio Roque. 2020. Let's do that first! a comparative analysis of instruction-giving in human-human and human-robot situated dialogue. In *Proceedings of the 24th Workshop on the Semantics and Pragmatics of Dialogue - Full Papers*, Virtually at Brandeis, Waltham, New Jersey. SEMDIAL.

Martin J. Pickering and Simon Garrod. 2004. Toward a mechanistic psychology of dialogue. *Behavioral and Brain Sciences*, 27(2):169–190.

Mirco Ravanelli, Titouan Parcollet, Aku Rouhe, Peter Plantinga, Elena Rastorgueva, Loren Lugosch, Nauman Dawalatabad, Chou Ju-Chieh, Abdel Heba, Francois Grondin, William Aris, Chien-Feng Liao, Samuele Cornell, Sung-Lin Yeh, Hwidong Na, Yan Gao, Szu-Wei Fu, Cem Subakan, Renato De Mori, and Yoshua Bengio. 2021. Speechbrain. `https://github.com/speechbrain/speechbrain`.

Sida I. Wang, Percy Liang, and Christopher D. Manning. 2016. Learning language games through interaction. In *Proceedings of the 54th Annual Meeting of the Association for Computational Linguistics (Volume 1: Long Papers)*, pages 2368–2378, Berlin, Germany. Association for Computational Linguistics.

Anthony Zhang. 2017. Speech recognition (version 3.8).

A Example User-Agent Interaction.

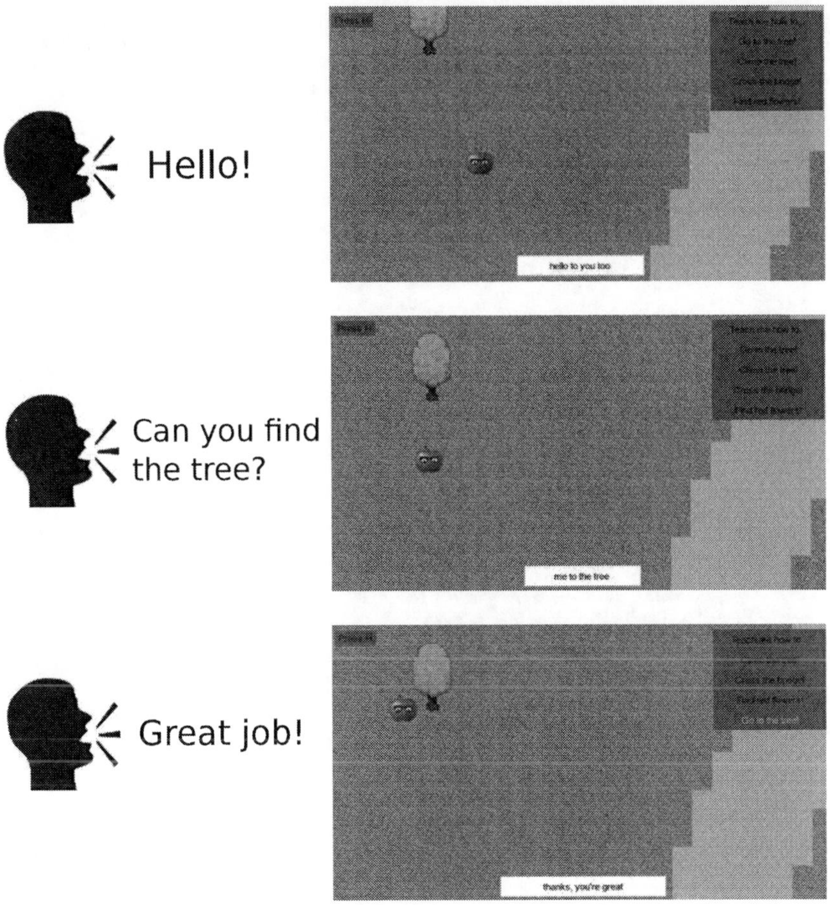

Figure 1: Example interaction.

B Example Instruction Processing.

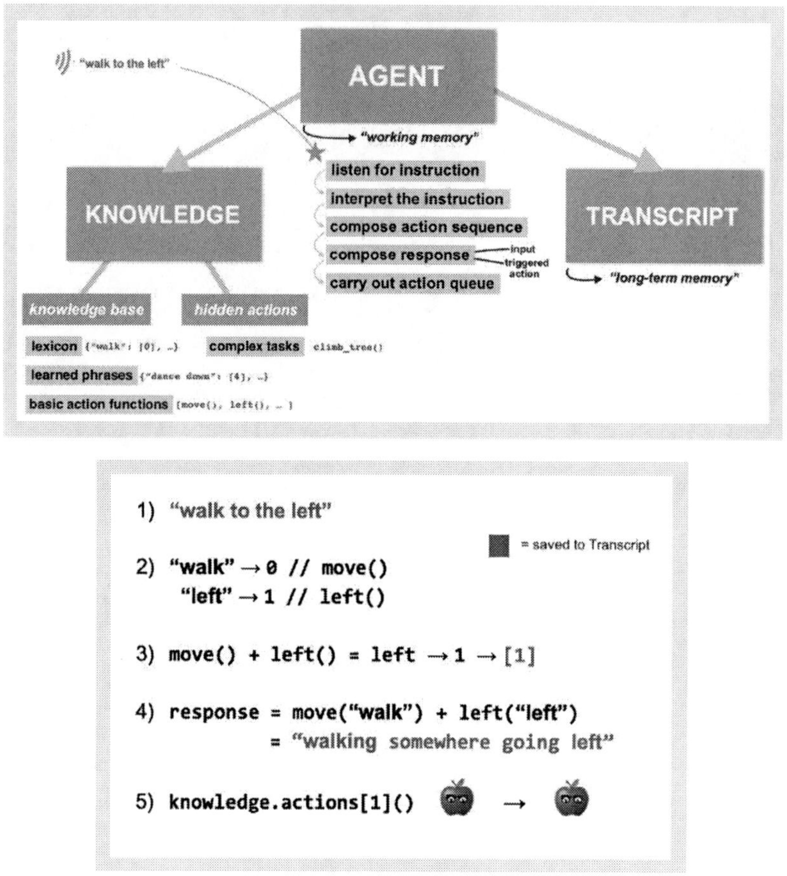

Figure 2: Agent processing of the instruction *walk to the left*.

C Transcripts.

Key_Pres	Instruction	Actions	Response	Task_Achieved	cle
SPACE	co-op	[]	how do I co-op?		
SPACE	go up	[[3]]	going somewhere going up		1
SPACE	club feather	[]	how do I club feather?		
SPACE	go up further	[[3]]	going somewhere going up	success: go to the tree	1
SPACE	go left	[[1]]	going somewhere going left		1
SPACE	go up	[[3]]	going somewhere going up	success: climb the tree	1
SPACE	go to the water	[[0]]	going somewhere		1
SPACE	go down	[[4]]	going somewhere going down		1
SPACE	go to the water	[[0]]	going somewhere		1
SPACE	headright	[]	how do I headright?		
SPACE	go to the right	[[2]]	going somewhere going right		1
SPACE	go right	[[2]]	going somewhere going right		1
SPACE	gopher the right	[[2]]	going right		
SPACE	keep going	[]	how do I keep going?		1
SPACE	keep going to the ride	[]	how do I keep going to the ride?		
SPACE	keep going to the right until you come to the wate	[[2], [8]]	going right me moving somewhere		1
SPACE	keep going	[]	how do I keep going?		1
SPACE	move to the right	[[2]]	moving somewhere going right		1
SPACE	can you find the bridge	[[8], [10]]	me to the bridge		1
SPACE	cross the bridge	[[10]]	to the bridge		1
SPACE	cross the bridge	[[10]]	to the bridge		1
SPACE	move across the bridge move right across the bi	[[10], [2], [10]]	moving somewhere to the bridge moving somewhere going right to the br		1
SPACE	thyroid	[]	how do I thyroid?		
SPACE	go to the right	[[2]]	going somewhere going right		1
SPACE	cross the bridge	[[10]]	to the bridge		1
SPACE	move to the other side of the bridge	[[10]]	moving somewhere to the bridge		1
SPACE	move to the other side of the river	[[0]]	moving somewhere		1
SPACE	move to the other end of the bridge	[[10]]	moving somewhere to the bridge		1
SPACE	move right	[[2]]	moving somewhere going right		1
SPACE	move right	[[2]]	moving somewhere going right		1
SPACE	move right	[[2]]	moving somewhere going right	success: cross the bri	1
SPACE	find red flowers	[]	how do I find red flowers?		1
SPACE	find flowers	[]	how do I find flowers?		1
SPACE	move right	[[2]]	moving somewhere going right		1
SPACE	move up	[[3]]	moving somewhere going up		1
SPACE	move all the way down	[[4]]	moving somewhere going down		1
SPACE	move down five times	[[4]]	moving somewhere going down		1
SPACE	move down 5 times	[[4]]	moving somewhere going down		1
SPACE	move down five times again	[[4]]	moving somewhere going down		1
SPACE	move right	[[2]]	moving somewhere going right		1
SPACE	move 9 steps to the right	[[2]]	moving somewhere going right		1
SPACE	move to the right to the red flowers	[[2]]	moving somewhere going right		1
SPACE	move further to the right	[[2]]	moving somewhere going right		1
SPACE	again	[]	how do I again?		1
SPACE	move to the right	[[2]]	moving somewhere going right		1
SPACE	move to the right	[[2]]	moving somewhere going right	success: find red flowe	1
SPACE	goodbye	[]	how do I goodbye?		1
SPACE	where are you	[[8]]	me		1
SPACE	esu	[]	how do I esu?		
SPACE	where are you	[[8]]	me		1

Figure 3: Transcript file of a completed game.

SHAPELURN:
An Interactive Language Learning Game with Logical Inference

Katharina Stein **Leonie Harter** **Luisa Geiger**
Department of Language Science and Technology
Saarland Informatics Campus
Saarland University, Germany
{kstein, leonieh, lgeiger}@coli.uni-saarland.de

Abstract

We investigate if a model can learn natural language with minimal linguistic input through interaction. Addressing this question, we design and implement an interactive language learning game that learns logical semantic representations compositionally. Our game allows us to explore the benefits of logical inference for natural language learning. Evaluation shows that the model can accurately narrow down potential logical representations for words over the course of the game, suggesting that our model is able to learn lexical mappings from scratch successfully.

1 Introduction

An open question in NLP research is how models can learn natural language most successfully and effectively. Many state-of-the-art semantic parsers and machine learning algorithms are dependent on large data sets for successful training. This poses a problem when using NLP applications for low-resource languages or specific domains for which only little annotated training data is available if any at all (Klie et al., 2020). *Interactive NLP Systems* can overcome these problems as they start with a small or even empty set of training data that gets extended based on user feedback for the predictions the model makes based on its current parameters (Lee et al., 2020). Therefore, learning mappings from natural language to formal representations through interaction with a user is an attractive approach for low-resource settings. The model parameters are optimized based on feedback and the resulting data itself can be used as training data for other models avoiding costly manual annotations.

However, the interaction with a not yet fully trained model can get monotonous or can lead to frustration on the part of the users if they do not benefit from the interaction themselves (Lee et al., 2020). Wang et al. (2016) present an interactive language learning setting, called SHRDLURN, in which a model learns a language by interacting with a player in a game environment, hence making the interactive learning setting more attractive and fun for users. Their model is language independent and can be taught any language from scratch.

Here we follow Wang et al. (2016) and design and implement an interactive language learning game where a model learns to map natural language to logical forms in a compositional way based on the feedback provided by the player[1]. Whereas Wang et al. (2016)'s model learns to map instructions to executable logical forms, we aim to learn logical formulas that evaluate to truth values with respect to the current state of the game environment. This decision was taken because the additional information about the truth can be incorporated in the parsing and learning process in order to already restrict the potential logical formulas. Overall, we are trying to answer the following research questions: Can we implement a model that 1) can learn a natural language from scratch only from interacting with a user and 2) is not dependent on any language specific syntax and is hence language independent.

2 Previous Work

Several approaches map natural language to logical form for its ability to model inferences. Zettlemoyer and Collins (2005) present a learning algorithm for mapping sentences to their lambda calculus semantic representations and automatically inducing a combinatory categorical grammar (CCG). Zettlemoyer and Collins (2007) extend this algorithm to make the grammar more flexible. Pasupat and Liang (2015) also present a flexible semantic parsing framework, the floating parser, for learning mappings from natural language to logical forms

[1]The complete code is available under https://github.com/itsLuisa/SHAPELURN

Proceedings of the First Workshop on Interactive Learning for Natural Language Processing , pages 16–24
August 5, 2021. ©2021 Association for Computational Linguistics

in the lambda dependency-based compositional semantic language (Liang, 2013). Liang and Potts (2015) present a framework for learning to map natural language utterances to logical forms that combines the principle of compositionality with a standard machine learning algorithm.

Current approaches that aim at overcoming the need for costful annotated training data include the interactive *human-in-the-loop* method where a human corrects annotations predicted by a machine learning system and this feedback is used to improve future predictions. Klie et al. (2020) use this approach for the task of Entity Linking and He et al. (2016) apply the approach to a CCG parser, thereby improving parsing performance. Goldwasser and Roth (2014) present a learning approach where a model learns to map natural language instructions to logical representations of solitaire game rules based on feedback. Finally, Zhang et al. (2018) present a game for grounded language acquisition where a human teaches an agent language from scratch in a natural language conversation.

3 From SHRDLURN to SHAPELURN

3.1 Game Design

Wang et al. (2016) designed their model to perform a block building task in 3-D space using natural language instructions from the player. The computer and player work together towards a shared goal (a specific block position) while only the player knows the goal and only the computer can move the blocks. The more successful the model learns the human's language, the faster this shared goal can be reached (Wang et al., 2016).

Based on this idea, we design a 2-D game environment where the model and player work towards teaching the model a language with the user giving descriptive input about the environment. The user is presented with a randomly generated picture displaying varying numbers of objects which have one of three shapes (circle, square, triangle) and one of four colors (red, blue, yellow, green) (see Figure 1). The picture corresponds to a 4×4-grid which is internally represented as a matrix allowing for simplified spatial calculations.

The user is asked to describe one or more of the displayed objects by typing in one phrase in a language of their choice. Importantly, this language should be kept consistent in order for the computer to recognize language specific patterns. The program proceeds by parsing the input into

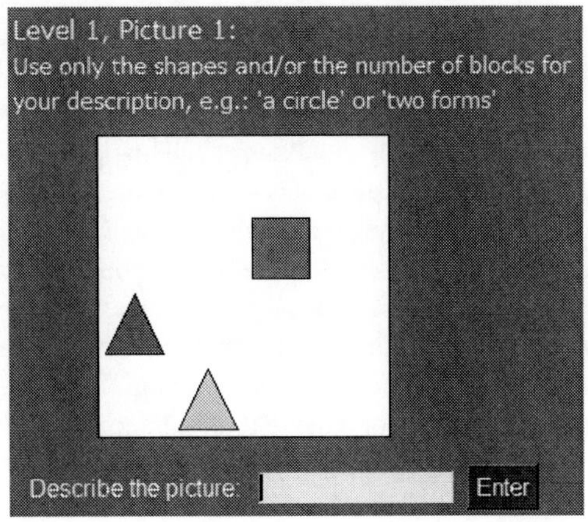

Figure 1: The interface displaying three randomly generated objects the user can use to build an utterance

a logical formula, comparing it to the matrix and then making a guess on which object(s) the user was referring to by marking them with a black border. The user can then provide feedback in terms of selecting the right marking by skipping through the computer's guesses which show up in descending order according to their probability (see A.1). Like this, the feedback is specific enough for the model to learn lexical mappings.

This process is repeated over 4 levels of alternating complexity (regarding both the number of displayed blocks and the length of the input) each consisting of 20 (level 2) or 15 (other levels) pictures. The learning algorithm is responsible for the guesses to improve as the game proceeds and lets the model adapt to the input language.

3.2 Preprocessing and Parsing

We tokenize, lowercase and stem the input, since learning is much quicker if it is clear that e.g. *triangle* and *triangles* refer to the same shape. In order to stem language independently, we use a cosine similarity based heuristic. To compare two tokens, we transform them into vectors with length of the longer one. If they have the same character at a position, the vectors get a 1 there. Otherwise one vector gets a 1 and the other a -1. If the cosine similarity of the vectors is > 0.65, we assume the tokens to belong to the same word (see Figure 2).

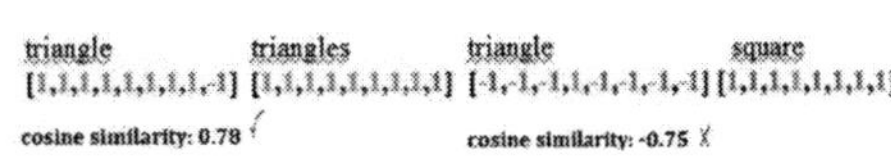

Figure 2: Two stemming examples

Since Liang and Potts (2015)'s framework[2], which we use as groundwork, employs a CYK parser that forces players to adhere to a strict syntax, we equipped it with Pasupat and Liang (2015)'s floating parser instead. This parser stores intermediate results in a chart according to their semantic category c and size s (Figure 3), but does not consider which indices the covered tokens span. This allows to parse syntactic structures without binding the user to a certain syntax. We adjust the three derivation rules for parsing to our grammar:

(1) $(TokenSpan, i, j)[s] \rightarrow (c, 1)[f]$

(2) $\emptyset \rightarrow (c, 1)[f]$

(3) $(c_1, s_1)[f_1] + (c_2, s_2)[f_2] \rightarrow (c, s_1 + s_2)[f_1(f_2)]$

Rule (1) is a lexical rule matching a token span from index i-j to a rule in the lexicon entry of the word in this span telling us which category c and which function f to use. Rule (2) allows us to establish lexical logical forms matching words we have not seen in the input and proceeds with these "imaginary tokens" as in (1). It is used to create the formula in the parse chart field (E,1) in Figure 3. Rule (3) combines parse items of categories the grammar allows to combine. We only allow each token to be used once per parse.

Previous work used beam search to address the huge number of possible parse trees (Wang et al., 2016; Pasupat and Liang, 2015). However, as beam search does not guarantee that the correct parse is kept we decided to not use a heuristic approach for pruning. Instead, we restrict the number of parses by building only formulas up to the size corresponding to the number of tokens in the input plus four. Additionally, we allow each token to be mapped to only one lexical rule per parse. This averts building non-sense constructions like *(exist([2])(blue(BF(triangle,all))))(exist([1])(blue(BF(square,all))))* for the utterance "two triangles and one blue square" (considering the picture in Figure 1).

	E	N	C	B	EN	BC	V
1	[exist]	[[1]]	[blue]	[BF(circle,all)]			
2					[exist([1])]	[blue(BF(circle,all))]	
4							[exist([1])(blue(BF(circle,all)))]

Figure 3: Parse Chart for "one blue circle"

3.3 Grammar

For our grammar we use the same overall structure as Liang and Potts (2015) (see A.3 for the complete grammar). The main information is encoded in the lexicon which is a dictionary that pairs words with a list of corresponding lexical rules. A lexical rule is a triple of a category (B, C, E, N, POS or CONJ), a logical form and a weight. For example, the word "red" is paired with (C, *red*, w), where C is the category, *red* the logical form as defined by the grammar and w the current weight.

The logical formulas for entries of category B and N are evaluated directly whereas the other logical forms are functions whose evaluation is specified separately using lambda calculus. For example, *red* is defined as the function $\lambda x(BF(red, x))$ where $BF(condition, list)$ is a function that yields all blocks from *list* that fulfill *condition*.

We use a set of binary CFG rules to define which categories can be combined and how logical formulas are applied to each other to yield larger formulas, e.g. BC $\rightarrow$ C B specifies that formulas of category C and B can be combined to a formula of category BC by applying C to B.

Each completed formula V is composed of at least one sub-formula of the categories B, N, E and C, and the categories POS and CONJ allow to build more complex formulas for inputs including relative positions and conjunctions.[3] Descriptions not specifying a color are handled by rule (2) of the floating parser that introduces a lexical rule of category C with an empty condition into the parse. For lower parsing complexity, users are instructed to mention only the objects, e.g. "a circle" instead of "there is a circle". We model the implicit existential quantification with a lexical rule for *exists* that gets introduced into each formula by rule (2).

3.4 Learning Algorithm

Like Wang et al. (2016), we aim to learn correct lexical rule(s) for all words in the lexicon. Initially, every new word gets paired with every lexical rule. Following Zettlemoyer and Collins (2005)'s approach in a simplified way, we delete the most unlikely pairs during training leaving the correct ones remain. We use Liang and Potts (2015)'s learning algorithm, a linear regression model optimized with stochastic gradient descent (SGD), which returns weight changes for word-rule pairs improving the model. Whereas Wang et al. (2016)'s features consist of n-grams and skip-grams for the utterance, tree-grams for the formulas and a formula depth,

[2] https://github.com/cgpotts/annualreview-complearning

[3] The denotation of a formula V consists of the truth of the description w.r.t. the picture and the list of blocks that make the description *true*.

our features only contain a list of word-rule pairs. This is sufficient, since the formula's structure and depth and the distances between combinable words are handled by the floating parser.

After a training round we get weight changes for all words in the input paired with the rules used to build the gold standard logical formulas and the ones predicted by the model. We sum up the weights for each pair after every training step. If a weight sum reaches the lower threshold of -0.1, we delete this rule for the corresponding word. If all pairs get weight change 0, SGD has converged, so the model is optimal for the current training batch. Hence, the word rule pairs used to build the formulas for the current training utterance must be the correct ones and all others can be deleted. If a weight sum reaches the upper threshold of 1.0, we assume this rule to be correct and delete all other rules for the word with weight sum ≤ 0.

As different formulas can have the same denotation (see Figure 4), we group all formulas evaluating to *true* by the guessed blocks they evaluate to. Only these guesses are then presented to the player. The formulas leading to the correct blocks, as determined by the user feedback, are used as gold standard training batch. During training we collate all possible parses. Otherwise too much information is lost, which causes deletions of correct rules. Liang and Potts (2015)'s cost function gave us too few weight changes $\neq 0$. Therefore, we average over all rules of a formula if this rule was also used in the gold formulas (value 1) or not (value 0):

$$\frac{1}{n}\sum_{i=1}^{n}\begin{cases}0 & if(w_i, r_i)\; in\; gold\; word\; rule\; pairs\\ 1 & otherwise\end{cases}$$

n: *number of tokens* w_i: *token number i*

r_i: *rule applied to* w_i *to get current formula*

gold word rule pairs: *word rule pairs leading to gold formula*

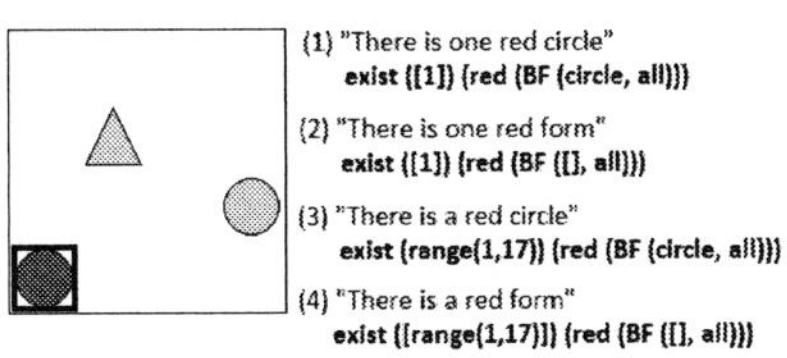

Figure 4: Four formulas with the same denotation

4 Evaluation

For a preliminary evaluation of the performance of the model we collected and analyzed data of seven participants who played the game in English (3), Spanish (1), German (2) and Esperanto (1). One of the participants completed two levels, four three levels and only two completed all four levels.

We planned to follow Wang et al. (2016) and count how often the user needs to click "NEXT" i.e. how far down the ranked parses the correct solution is. For our project to be viewed as successful, this number should decrease over the course of the game. Due to the simple game design, the exclusion of formulas evaluating to *false* and the grouping of identical markings, the total number possible markings is very low throughout the whole game and so is the number of clicks needed to arrive at the desired one ($M = 1.27$). But because of our simplified game setting, this cannot be directly compared to Wang et al. (2016)'s results. Since the number of clicks almost does not change in our case, it is not a meaningful measure for evaluating the improvement of the model.

To assess performance within the model itself, we analyze the remaining rules for each word. Initially, there are 20 possible rules per word as each new word gets paired with each rule from the lexicon and ideally exactly the correct rule(s) for each word should be left finally. Figure 5 shows the average number of rules per word left after each level. As our data set is very small the results have to be taken with a grain of salt. Nevertheless, the plot reveals that the model was able to decrease the number of possible rules per word by about 15 (see A.2). Manual investigation of the remaining rules at the end of level 3 revealed a total of 1202 deletions (63.9%), out of which only seven were falsely deleted (0.58%). This indicates that our model is able to successfully exclude incorrect mappings.

5 Discussion

Although, the setting of our language learning game is simpler than SHRDLURN, the 2-D grid environment allows to elicit different kinds of inputs that involve the composition of colors and shapes as well as relative spatial relations between objects that can be nested. In contrast to Wang et al. (2016), the player task in our game is not to give instructions to reach a specified goal state from the current state but to describe some part of the current state of the game (picture). Although

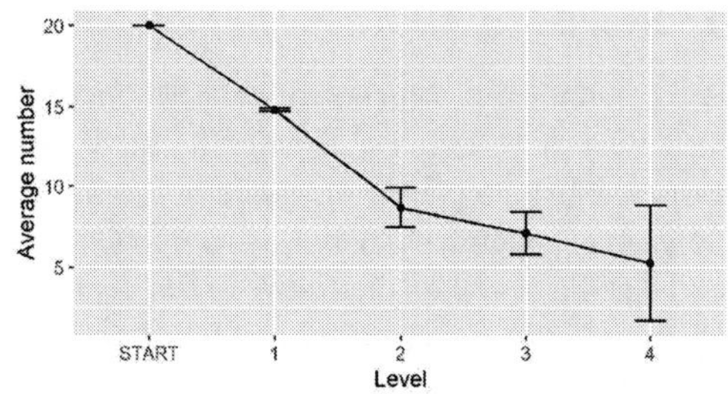

Figure 5: Mean number of rules per word left after each level. Error bars indicate 95% confidence intervals.

we restrict the complexity of the descriptions in the first levels to improve the first learning phase, the player task is in general a very open task as there are many ways to describe objects in a grid and the player can freely choose the objects to describe as well as the properties used to reference them. This makes the setting particularly interactive and allows to investigate in which ways humans choose and formulate their descriptions.

The design of the player task allows us to use the truth values of the parses in order to present only the *true* guesses to the player. Hence, the number of potential denotations is limited by the number of possibilities to mark different combinations of objects in the picture. This decreases the number of denotations the player can choose from compared to Wang et al. (2016) where the number of potential successor states for a current state is much higher. Although our design inhibits to use the number of clicks during the game as evaluation measurement, we see the overall low number of guesses as an advantage: the player spends less time on clicking through wrong guesses even in cases where the correct denotation is ranked very low what can improve the playing and success experience.

We find that the informativeness of feedback plays a crucial role in interactive learning. Our results indicate that making the current "knowledge" of the computer as explicit as possible, e.g. by marking all blocks mentioned in the input, could be a promising starting point as simple user feedback can provide enough information for learning.

During testing we found that the learning progress depends on specific combinations of descriptions and pictures. Learning appears to benefit from situations where the correct formula for the description differs in one lexical rule from other *true* parses: "a red circle" is more informative with respect to the meaning of "red" for a picture that shows a red circle and a circle in another color than for a picture displaying only one (red) circle.

The main advantage of using only input from the player to train the model is its independence of the availability of (annotated) training data as opposed to approaches requiring large data sets such as neural approaches. Hence, our approach is applicable for low resource settings. However, our model requires a grammar that covers all semantic concepts that can be part of the interaction. Due to our game design, the number of concepts our grammar needs to address is very limited but extending the domain requires increasing the number of handwritten rules. Therefore, scaling the model to larger domains would require the costful construction of a large-scale grammar.

Concerning the scalability of the game environment, the model could be easily adjusted to create more complex pictures as long as an adequate internal representation is found.

A key challenge of our work was the high uncertainty of the model. The computer has no initial knowledge about language and must consider each lexicon entry for each word. Additionally, the floating parser can combine the corresponding logical formulas in any order, discard tokens from the input and add additional logical forms. The number of parses is thus huge for short sentences and grows exponentially with sentence length, vastly increasing parsing and learning times. Future work could use beam search at higher levels to handle this.

6 Conclusion

We implement an interactive language learning game where the computer learns natural language based on user feedback. We find that learning interactively from scratch with a language independent model is complex due to the huge number of potential parses. Our results indicate that our model is able to learn language through interaction and low-resource domains and languages could benefit from such an approach. Future work will address the trade-off between increasing flexibility and increasing processing times.

Acknowledgments

We would like to thank Dr. Lucia Donatelli for the valuable discussions and support throughout the project development and writing process. Further, we would like to express our gratitude towards the participants of our evaluation experiment.

References

Dan Goldwasser and Dan Roth. 2014. Learning from natural instructions. *Machine learning*, 94(2):205–232.

Luheng He, Julian Michael, Mike Lewis, and Luke Zettlemoyer. 2016. Human-in-the-loop parsing. In *Proceedings of the 2016 Conference on Empirical Methods in Natural Language Processing*, pages 2337–2342, Austin, Texas. Association for Computational Linguistics.

Jan-Christoph Klie, Richard Eckart de Castilho, and Iryna Gurevych. 2020. From Zero to Hero: Human-In-The-Loop Entity Linking in Low Resource Domains. In *Proceedings of the 58th Annual Meeting of the Association for Computational Linguistics*, pages 6982–6993, Online. Association for Computational Linguistics.

Ji-Ung Lee, Christian M. Meyer, and Iryna Gurevych. 2020. Empowering Active Learning to Jointly Optimize System and User Demands. In *Proceedings of the 58th Annual Meeting of the Association for Computational Linguistics*, pages 4233–4247, Online. Association for Computational Linguistics.

Percy Liang. 2013. Lambda dependency-based compositional semantics. *arXiv preprint arXiv:1309.4408*.

Percy Liang and Christopher Potts. 2015. Bringing machine learning and compositional semantics together. *Annual Review of Linguistics*, 1(1):355–376.

Panupong Pasupat and Percy Liang. 2015. Compositional semantic parsing on semi-structured tables. In *Proceedings of the 53rd Annual Meeting of the Association for Computational Linguistics and the 7th International Joint Conference on Natural Language Processing (Volume 1: Long Papers)*, pages 1470–1480, Beijing, China. Association for Computational Linguistics.

Sida I. Wang, Percy Liang, and Christopher D. Manning. 2016. Learning language games through interaction. In *Proceedings of the 54th Annual Meeting of the Association for Computational Linguistics (Volume 1: Long Papers)*, pages 2368–2378, Berlin, Germany. Association for Computational Linguistics.

Luke S. Zettlemoyer and Michael Collins. 2005. Learning to map sentences to logical form: Structured classification with probabilistic categorial grammars. In *Proceedings of the Twenty-First Conference on Uncertainty in Artificial Intelligence*, UAI'05, page 658–666, Arlington, Virginia, USA. AUAI Press.

Luke S. Zettlemoyer and Michael Collins. 2007. Online learning of relaxed ccg grammars for parsing to logical form. In *Proceedings of the 2007 Joint Conference on Empirical Methods in Natural Language Processing and Computational Natural Language Learning (EMNLP-CoNLL)*, pages 678–687.

Haichao Zhang, Haonan Yu, and Wei Xu. 2018. Interactive language acquisition with one-shot visual concept learning through a conversational game. *arXiv preprint arXiv:1805.00462*.

A Appendices

A.1 Game Design

Level	Instruction
0	Welcome to SHAPELURN, where you can teach the computer any language of your choice! You will be looking at different pictures and describing them to the computer in one sentence. There will be four levels with different constraints on the descriptions. Please use short sentences in the first two levels and do not use negation at all.
1	Use only the shapes and/or the number of blocks for your description e.g.: *'a circle'* or *'two forms'*
2	You can additionally describe the blocks by color e.g: *'two blue forms'*
3	Now you can describe relations between blocks and use conjunction (please don't use colors) e.g.: *'a circle under a square'*
4	Describe whatever you want!

Table 1: The overall instructions for the input descriptions (0) and the level specific constraints for the descriptions.

Figure 6 - 8 illustrate the course of the game for an example picture and the input description "two triangles". The user is shown a picture and enters a description. Then the computer makes a guess and the user clicks NEXT until the correct guess is shown.

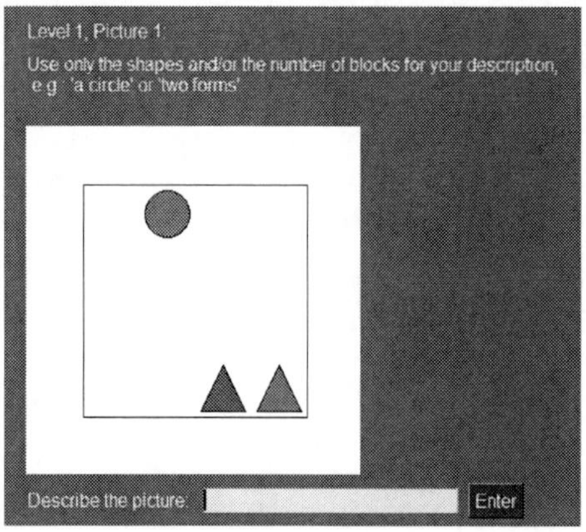

Figure 6: Grid generated by the model in level 1

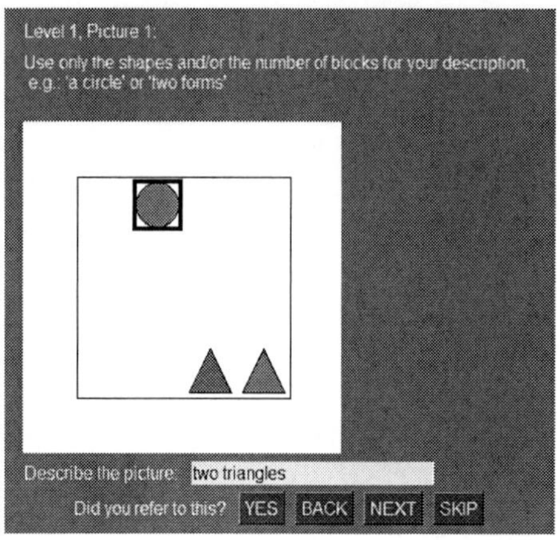

Figure 7: First guess of the model, user clicks NEXT

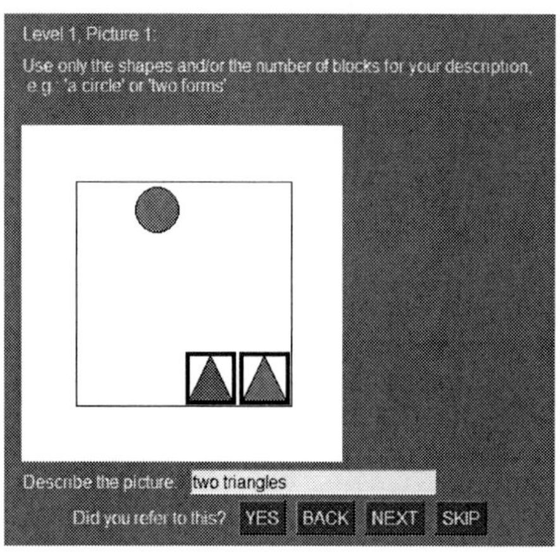

Figure 8: Next guess is correct, user clicks YES

A.2 Evaluation

Level	Mean	SD	Participants
1	14.801	0.114	7
2	8.691	1.319	7
3	7.116	1.250	6
4	5.280	0.396	2

Table 2: Mean and sd for the average number of rules per word in the lexicon at the end of each level

A.3 The Grammar

	Rule
1	V → EN BC
2	V → CONJ_1 V
3	CONJ_1 → CONJ V
4	EN → E N
5	BC → C B
6	BC → POS_NB BC
7	POS_NB → POS_N BC
8	POS_N → POS N

Table 3: The rules of the CFG grammar used to derive the input utterances and the logical forms

	Lexical Rule: (category, logical form, weight)	Example Word
1	(B, $BF([\lambda b(b.shape == "rectangle")], all), w)$	"square"
2	(B, $BF([\lambda b(b.shape == "circle")], all), w)$	"circle"
3	(B, $BF([\lambda b(b.shape == "triangle")], all), w)$	"triangle"
4	(B, $BF([\ \ ], all), w)$	"form"
5	(N, $range(1, 17), w)$	"a"
6	(N, $[1], w)$	"one"
7	(N, $[2], w)$	"two"
8	(N, $[3], w)$	"three"
9	(C, $green, w)$	"green"
10	(C, $blue, w)$	"blue"
11	(C, $yellow, w)$	"yellow"
12	(C, $red, w)$	"red"
13	(POS, $over, w)$	"over"
14	(POS, $under, w)$	"under"
15	(POS, $next, w)$	"next [to]"
16	(POS, $left, w)$	"[to the] left [of]"
17	(POS, $right, w)$	"[to the] right [of]"
18	(CONJ, $und, w)$	"and"
19	(CONJ, $oder, w)$	"or"
20	(CONJ, $xoder, w)$	"or"
21	(C, $anycol, w)$	$\emptyset$
22	(E, $exist, w)$	$\emptyset$ / [there is]

Function $BF(condition, all)$ returns all blocks from the list of all blocks of the picture that fulfill condition $condition$

Table 4: The lexicon of the grammar where each lexical rule is triple of (category, logical form, weight) and English example words for each rule.

	Logical Form from Lexicon	Function for interpretation
1	$exist$	$\lambda n(\lambda b(update\_guess(b)\ and\ len(b)\ in\ n))$
2	$green$	$\lambda x(BF([\lambda b(b.color == "green")], x))$
3	$blue$	$\lambda x(BF([\lambda b(b.color == "blue")], x))$
4	$yellow$	$\lambda x(BF([\lambda b(b.color == "yellow")], x))$
5	red	$\lambda x(BF([\lambda b(b.color == "red")], x))$
6	$anycol$	$\lambda x(BF([\ ], x))$
7	$over$	$\lambda n(\lambda x(\lambda y(PT(y, x, n, "o"))))$
8	$under$	$\lambda n(\lambda x(\lambda y(PT(y, x, n, "u"))))$
9	$next$	$\lambda n(\lambda x(\lambda y(PT(y, x, n, "n"))))$
10	$left$	$\lambda n(\lambda x(\lambda y(PT(y, x, n, "l"))))$
11	$right$	$\lambda n(\lambda x(\lambda y(PT(y, x, n, "r"))))$
12	und	$\lambda v1(\lambda v2(v1\ and\ v2))$
13	$oder$	$\lambda v1(\lambda v2(v1\ or\ v2))$
14	$xoder$	$\lambda v1(\lambda v2((v1\ and\ not\ v2) or (v2\ and\ not\ v1))))$

Function $BF(condition, x)$ returns all blocks from the list x that fulfill condition $condition$

Function $PT(y, x, n, "pos")$ returns all blocks from the list y that stand in position $"pos"$ to n blocks from list x

Function $update\_guess(b)$ returns a list of all mentioned blocks by recursively backtracking from the blocks in list b

Table 5: The functions used to interpret the logical forms for the categories E, C, POS and CONJ.

	CFG	Logical Form	Denotation
1	B → circle	*BF*(circle, all)	the list with all blocks of the picture with shape circle
2	N → one	[1]	[1]
3	C → blue	*blue*	the *C* s.t. *C*(x) returns a list of all blocks of x with color blue
4	POS → over	*over*	the *POS* s.t. *POS*(y)(x)(n) returns the sublist of blocks from y that are located over n blocks from x
5	E → ∅	*exist*	the *E* s.t. *E*(b)(n) returns True if length of b satisfies n and False otherwise
6	BC → C B	*C*(B)	application of denotation of *C* to denotation of B
7	V → EN BC	*EN*(BC)	application of denotation of *EN* to denotation of *BC*
8	EN → E N	*E*(n)	application of denotation of *E* to denotation of n

Input utterance: "one blue square over a red triangle"

Logical Form: $exist([1])(over(range(1, 17))(blue(BF(square, all)))(red(BF(triangle, all))))$

Denotation: True and the list of guessed blocks consisting of the blue square and the red triangle

Table 6: Illustration of the way in which the grammar works for the example "[there is] one blue square over a red triangle". The upper part shows the lexical rules and the mid part the combination rules needed for the example sentence. The lower part shows the input utterance with its simplified logical form and the corresponding denotation with respect to the picture in Figure 1 in the paper.

A Proposal: Interactively Learning to Summarise Timelines by Reinforcement Learning

Yuxuan Ye
Intelligent Systems Laboratory
University of Bristol
yuxuan.ye@bristol.ac.uk

Edwin Simpson
Intelligent Systems Laboratory
University of Bristol
edwin.simpson@bristol.ac.uk

Abstract

Timeline Summarisation (TLS) aims to generate a concise, time-ordered list of events described in sources such as news articles. However, current systems do not provide an adequate way to adapt to new domains nor to focus on the aspects of interest to a particular user. Therefore, we propose a method for interactively learning abstractive TLS using Reinforcement Learning (RL). We define a compound reward function and use RL to fine-tune an abstractive Multi-document Summarisation (MDS) model, which avoids the need to train using reference summaries. One of the sub-reward functions will be learned interactively from user feedback to ensure the consistency between users' demands and the generated timeline. The other sub-reward functions contribute to topical coherence and linguistic fluency. We plan experiments to evaluate whether our approach could generate accurate and precise timelines tailored for each user.

1 Introduction

Notable events often happen over a long period. For example, COVID-19 caused immeasurable damage around the world, lasting for more than a year. When reviewing different aspects of the disaster, the huge number of reports and news articles makes it difficult to trace the development of events such as outbreaks, policy interventions and vaccination efforts. TLS can solve this problem by identifying significant dates and summarising events of sub-topics.

Most prior TLS works focused on producing *extractive* timelines, which copies the original sentences from input documents (Martschat and Markert, 2018; Nguyen et al., 2014; Yan et al., 2011). Irrelevant and repeated information may be extracted in this process, decreasing the quality of the generated timelines. Abstractive timeline summarisation methods can address this problem (Steen and Markert, 2019; Barros et al., 2019) but few neural network models have been proposed due to the lack of reference timelines for supervised learning. Producing reference timelines by human requires expertise to capture important temporal information and sub-events from the source documents, thus it is extremely expensive. In MDS tasks, researchers have tried heuristics-based and unsupervised methods to address the reference data shortage problem (Ryang and Abekawa, 2012; Rioux et al., 2014). However, their results on some evaluation metrics, like ROUGE-2, only reached half of the upper bound. Gao et al. (2018) showed that interactive learning could improve the performance of an MDS system via leveraging users' preference, which is relatively easy to obtain, and does not require reference summaries. Therefore, we take inspiration from their work to propose an interaction-based abstractive TLS framework.

Martschat and Markert (2018) treated the TLS task as an MDS task and proposed a modular summarisation method, which achieved the state of the art and is adaptable. However, its adaptation requires abstracting mathematical constraints from concrete requirements. This contrasts with interactive learning (IL), which greatly decreases the cognitive burden for humans by receiving user feedback to refine summaries (Gao et al., 2018; Lin et al., 2010). Comparing to traditional approaches, interaction enables the model to learn from the users, thus it is possible to accurately tailor and refine timeline summaries according to users' demands.

In this paper, we propose an interaction-based abstractive timeline summarisation framework using deep RL. By learning a reward signal from user feedback, we can fine-tune a pretrained MDS model for the TLS task via a small number of interactive learning rounds. Therefore, our frame-

Proceedings of the First Workshop on Interactive Learning for Natural Language Processing , pages 25–31
August 5, 2021. ©2021 Association for Computational Linguistics

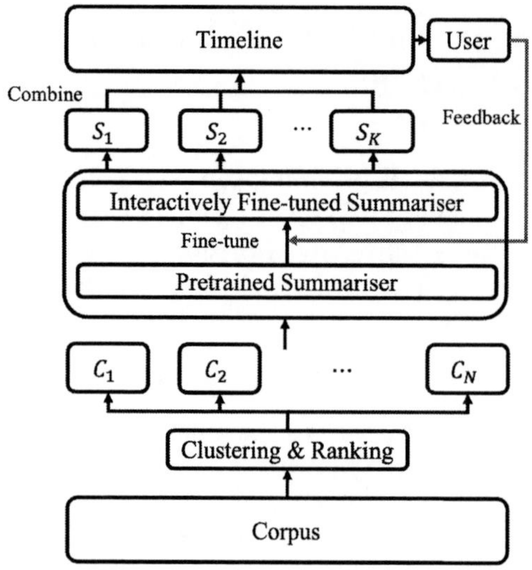

Figure 1: The workflow of our event detection timeline summarisation method

work should be capable of generating timeline summaries with high text quality after enough episodes of training. And we plan both simulation and real-user experiments to evaluate the framework on two benchmark TLS datasets, Timeline17 (Binh Tran et al., 2013; Tran et al., 2013) and Crisis (Tran et al., 2015).

The workflow of our model (Figure 1) mainly follows the event detection method, CLUST (Ghalandari and Ifrim, 2020), which identifies sub-events first and then generates summaries for them. Due to the RL-based interactive learning process in the framework, our model can be automatically adapted to new topics and adjusted by users' interests.

1. Firstly, we embed source documents into vectors and cluster them in vector space. Each cluster represents a sub-event in a large topic;

2. In the next step, we assign a date to each cluster. And they will be ranked by a metric to identify important sub-events;

3. Then it comes to our RL-based interactive learning process.

   (a) An abstractive MDS model will generate summaries for each sub-event. All summaries will be ordered by date to form a timeline.

   (b) The user can preview the timeline in this step and respond by expressing preferences over keywords or by comparing the new summary to an earlier version.

   (c) Using a reward function that evaluates the consistency between the produced timeline and those user preferences, offline RL then tunes the model and starts another round of interactive learning.

Our main contribution is a proposed interactive method for generating timelines for news, which adapts to user feedback through RL fine-tuning.

2 Related Work

Extractive Timeline Summarisation Prior extractive methods (Martschat and Markert, 2018; Ghalandari, 2017) defined several objective functions to assess the quality of timelines, including coverage of summaries and temporal information. These methods greedily select one sentence in each iteration to maximise the combined objective function. Our reward function is also modular but lacks monotonicity and submodularity, hence we use RL instead of a greedy algorithm.

Interactive Summarisation Instead of producing reference texts by crowdsourcing, obtaining information (e.g., keywords) via user interaction can be more practical to obtain training data. Liu et al. (2012) outperformed previous extractive MDS approaches on ROUGE-based metrics by querying topic words from users. Gao et al. (2018) collected pairwise comparisons between summaries from simulated users, which are then used to train a ranker without any reference data, and fixed the efficiency issue of IL. Due to the similarity between the MDS and TLS task, IL is expected to solve the reference timelines shortage problem as well, without increasing many computation expenses. So we introduce interaction into an RL-based TLS model for the first time.

Reinforcement Learning in Natural Language Generation (NLG) Recent research on applying RL on NLG tasks has received some success. Some prior works on dialogue systems (Song et al., 2020; Mesgar et al., 2020) utilized RL-based fine-tuning method to ensure the factual consistency of the response. In automatic summarisation (Gao et al., 2018, 2019; Simpson et al., 2020), IL is applied to learn a reward function from users, so that RL agents could learn a policy to summarise text indirectly under users' guidance. However, for the

TLS task, we are the first to use RL to generate summaries for key dates.

3 Method

All components of our method shown in Figure 1 will be introduced below.

3.1 Event Detection Timeline Summarisation

Clustering For each input document, we use the sentence-transformer (Reimers and Gurevych, 2019) based on DistilRoBERTa (Liu et al., 2019) to embed its sentences. Then we represent the document by the mean of the sentence vectors expecting that dense vectors could capture more information in text than TF-IDF vectors, as used in Steen and Markert (2019) and Ghalandari and Ifrim (2020).

Next, we use Affinity Propagation (AP) (Frey and Dueck, 2007) to cluster all the documents. AP is an unsupervised method, which automatically determines the number of clusters. AP uses an affinity matrix A, constructed by the Euclidean distance of each pair of document vectors.

To detect events accurately, we add constraints to the clustering algorithm. If two reports were published too apart from each other, although, with a small distance in vector space, they should be considered to belong to two similar but different sub-topics. In our model, we keep the setting of prior work (Steen and Markert, 2019). If d_i and d_j were published no more than t day(s) apart, $A_{i,j} = -\|\vec{d_i} - \vec{d_j}\|_2^{1/2}$, otherwise it will be assigned by 0.

Date Assignment By clustering all the documents, reports describing the same event are gathered. However, temporal information is equally as important as summaries in TLS, which differs from MDS. Martschat and Markert (2018) and Chen et al. (2019) adapted MDS methods to make them temporally sensitive. Both received outstanding results. In our work, we use HeidelTime (Strötgen and Gertz, 2015) to identify and count date expressions in documents. Following Ghalandari and Ifrim (2020), we assign each cluster with the most frequently mentioned date in it.

Cluster Ranking Some clusters contain less important information than others. According to Ghalandari and Ifrim (2020), the importance of a cluster is in proportion to the number of sentences that mentions the assigned date to some extent. To capture useful information, we use the same setting and only summarise the top-k important clusters.

Cluster Summarisation & Timeline Construction Summarising the sub-topic of a key date can be regarded as an MDS task, as each event has multiple sources. We plan to fine-tune an abstractive MDS model for this task, which will be introduced later. After all the top-k clusters are summarised, we combine all the summaries by date to generate a timeline. We follow the setting of Ghalandari and Ifrim (2020), which skips a cluster when its date is already used by another prior cluster.

3.2 Interaction

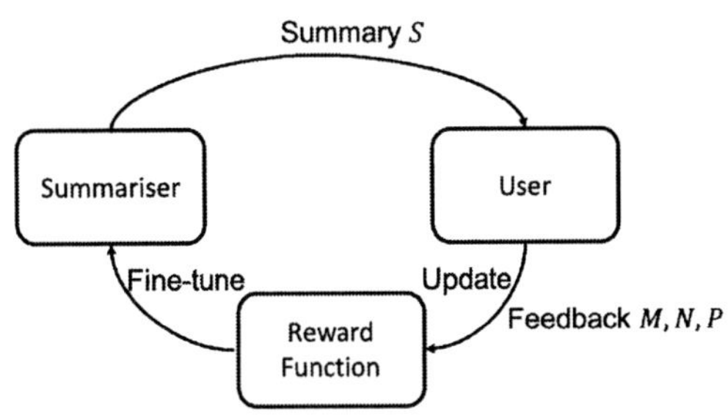

Figure 2: A view of interaction process

Every time the timeline is generated, the user can preview it and provide several types of feedback such as keywords and dates that must be included or excluded, and expressing preferences against previous version of the timeline. Given these feedback, we can renew our reward function and fine-tune the summariser via hundreds of RL episodes. Then we can produce a new timeline to start another round of interactive learning. After several interactive learning rounds, our model would be able to generate and tailor a high-quality timeline for the user.

3.3 RL-based fine-tuning

Timeline17		
	AR-F1	AR-F2
CLUST	0.082	0.02
PEGASUS-Multi_News	**0.089**	0.019

Table 1: Performance of two methods evaluated by Alignment ROUGE-1 and Alignment ROUGE-2.

PEGASUS We use PEGASUS (Zhang et al., 2020) to solve the MDS task on each cluster. PEGASUS is an abstractive summariser providing various fine-tuned versions. PEGASUS-Multi_News is fine-tuned on Multi-News (Fabbri et al., 2019) to summarise news articles. We found that PEGASUS-Multi_News outperforms the state-of-the-art extractive event detection method, CLUST (Ghalandari and Ifrim, 2020), when applying it directly on clusters without fine-tuning (Table 1). Therefore, it provides a strong basis for our following work.

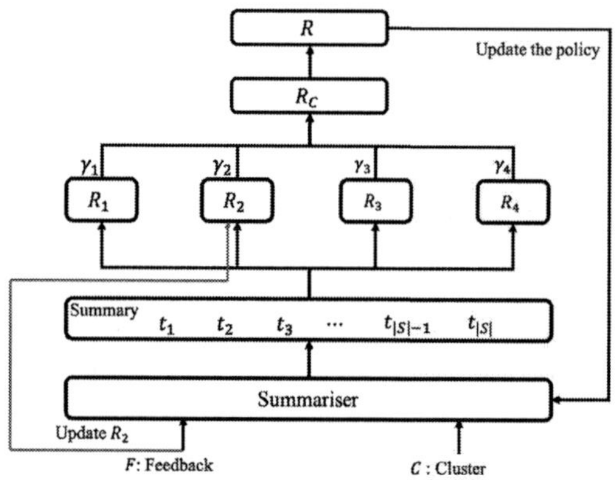

Figure 3: A view of our RL method

PEGASUS-RL Although PEGASUS is powerful enough to generate high-quality summaries, we still need RL to ensure the summaries are topically coherent and linguistically fluent. The PEGASUS model generates summaries token-by-token. When the last token, i.e. $\langle$eos$\rangle$, is generated, the reward component will assess the quality of the summary and produce a reward signal to update the summarising policy (Figure 3). This whole process will tune the parameters of PEGASUS so that it enhances the quality of the generated summary as well.

Action and Reward Function Let $D = (d_1, d_2, \ldots, d_{|D|})$ be a document cluster describing the same sub-topic. $P = (p_1, p_2, \ldots, p_{|P|})$ denotes the preferences between different versions of the generated timelines. Assuming that $p_1, p_2, \ldots, p_{|P|}$ are several different pairwise labels, collected over a number of rounds, comparing several different versions of the timeline. The words, dates and keyphrases that the user wants to include and exclude are marked as $M = (m_1, m_2, \ldots, m_{|M|})$ and $N = (n_1, n_2, \ldots, n_{|N|})$ individually. And $S = (t_1, t_2, \ldots, t_{|S|})$ is the summary generated for cluster D. Our goal is to fine-tune a single model to generate a summary S, for each cluster D that is linguistically fluent and topically coherent with any d_i and consistent with any piece of feedback p_i, m_i, n_i.

We regard each token generation process in Figure 3 as an action of PEGASUS. Our model is expected to generate a summary with topical coherence, linguistic fluency and consistency with the user's demands for each cluster. Thus, a compound reward function is proposed, which consists of four sub-reward functions: R_1 guarantees topical coherence with the cluster, R_2 enforces consistency with each piece of individual user feedback, R_3 and R_4 contribute to the linguistic fluency of the produced summaries. The reward of the cluster D is the weighted sum of them.

$$R_C = \gamma_1 R_1 + \gamma_2 R_2 + \gamma_2 R_3 + \gamma_4 R_4 \quad (1)$$

where $\gamma_{1,2,3,4}$ are the normalization factors that sum to one. The whole training signal R is the sum of k selected clusters' rewards.

Topical coherence sub-reward (R_1 and R_2) Topical coherence is the pivotal property of a summary. We measure how topically coherent the summary S is with a cluster D by their cosine similarity.

$$R_1 = \cos(\vec{S}, \vec{D}) \quad (2)$$

R_2 is the core reward function in the fine-tuning process, which will be updated in each interactive learning round. We embed all the keywords in M and N to dense vectors and measure their topic coherence by cosine similarities. Due to N represents the words that the user wants to exclude, we set its reward to be negative. To accommodate pairwise preference labels, we learn a ranking function using a random utility model (Thurstone, 1927; Mosteller, 2006). This provides a scoring function that should also be added to R_2.

$$\begin{aligned} R_2 = & w_1 score(\vec{S}, \vec{P}) \\ & + w_2 \sum_{m_i \in M} \cos(\vec{S}, \vec{m_i}) \\ & - w_3 \sum_{n_i \in N} \cos(\vec{S}, \vec{n_i}) \end{aligned} \quad (3)$$

where $w_{1,2,3}$ are the normalization factors.

Linguistic fluency sub-reward (R_3 and R_4) Prior work (Mesgar et al., 2020) has shown that applying RL to improve evaluation metrics' results might lead to decreasing in linguistic quality. To avoid that, we apply two sub-reward functions to our model. R_3 utilizes a language model which has been fine-tuned on a similar news dataset:

$$R_3 = \frac{\alpha - N(S)}{\alpha} \tag{4}$$

where $N(\cdot)$ is the Negative Log-likelihood loss function, and α is the maximum of $N(\cdot)$ so that it can normalize R_3. R_4 reduces repeated words in summaries, by penalizing repeated unigrams:

$$R_4 = 1 - \frac{\#repeated\_tokens\_in\_summary}{\#tokens\_in\_summary} \tag{5}$$

Training In this work, RL attempts to learn a policy P_θ that generates a summary maximizing the expectation of the reward function.

$$L = E_{S \sim P_\theta}[R(S, (C, F))] \tag{6}$$

However, RL is known for high variance issue when sampling the gradient. To solve this problem, we plan to run several hundred episodes of RL to increase the size of the sample and reduce the variance.

In addition, according to Mnih et al. (2016) and Mesgar et al. (2020), we can tune the policy function by actor-critic, which could further reduce variance in learning. In actor-critic algorithm, the policy function P_θ is regarded as the actor, and we define the residual of temporal difference Ψ_t to be the critic. Although Ψ_t is a biased estimation of the reward function R, we can reduce the variance via replacing the reward function R in the policy gradient equation (7) by Ψ_t, as in the following:

$$g = E\left[\sum_{t=0} \Psi_t \nabla_\theta \log P_\theta(a_t|s_t)\right] \tag{7}$$

4 Plan for Evaluation

As a kind of summarisation task, correctly extracting temporal information is the special challenge of TLS, which makes the evaluation more complex as well. In our work, we plan to evaluate our model by the suitable evaluation metrics proposed by Martschat and Markert (2017).

Concatenation ROUGE Discard all dates and concatenate all summaries in the reference and the output timeline. Evaluate ROUGE on two concatenated texts.

Alignment ROUGE Align the output timeline with the reference by the similarity and distance of their dates and apply ROUGE on them. Aligned summaries with distant dates will be penalized.

User feedback will be generated through mixed simulations, as in Gao et al. (2019) and studies with real users. Simulations will rely on references, from which keywords and dates can be extracted. Pairwise preferences can be simulated by comparing two summaries to a reference using ROUGE and selecting the highest-scoring summary. The system will be tested with different feedback types (keywords, dates, inclusion/exclusion, and preferences) to determine whether these forms of interaction are feasible to improve the summaries. However, the simulated user labels will be noisy, so we intend to evaluate with real users once we have developed a working system.

5 Summary

We propose an interactive method to summarise timelines without reference data. In each interactive learning round, we first update the reward function, and then use RL to fine-tune a huge neural network model. Then the model will generate summaries for each of the important sub-events, which are identified by textual similarity to the articles in the corpus. All the summaries will be ordered by their assigned dates to form a timeline. The user can preview the timeline and give feedback to start another round of interactive learning. Part of our method has been implemented, including PEGASUS to summarise event clusters but without RL or user feedback. Given the current experiment results, we can expect better performance after the interaction part implemented. The challenge remains in RL and designing suitable modes of interaction. We will move forward to our planned experiments and report our results in future work.

References

Cristina Barros, Elena Lloret, Estela Saquete, and Borja Navarro-Colorado. 2019. Natsum: Narrative abstractive summarization through cross-document timeline generation. *Information Processing & Management*, 56(5):1775–1793.

Giang Binh Tran, Mohammad Alrifai, and Dat Quoc Nguyen. 2013. Predicting relevant news events for timeline summaries. In *Proceedings of the 22nd International Conference on World Wide Web*, pages 91–92.

Xiuying Chen, Zhangming Chan, Shen Gao, Meng-Hsuan Yu, Dongyan Zhao, and Rui Yan. 2019. Learning towards abstractive timeline summarization. In *IJCAI*, pages 4939–4945.

Alexander R Fabbri, Irene Li, Tianwei She, Suyi Li, and Dragomir R Radev. 2019. Multi-news: A large-scale multi-document summarization dataset and abstractive hierarchical model. *arXiv preprint arXiv:1906.01749*.

Brendan J Frey and Delbert Dueck. 2007. Clustering by passing messages between data points. *science*, 315(5814):972–976.

Yang Gao, Christian M Meyer, and Iryna Gurevych. 2018. April: Interactively learning to summarise by combining active preference learning and reinforcement learning. *arXiv preprint arXiv:1808.09658*.

Yang Gao, Christian M Meyer, Mohsen Mesgar, and Iryna Gurevych. 2019. Reward learning for efficient reinforcement learning in extractive document summarisation. *arXiv preprint arXiv:1907.12894*.

Demian Gholipour Ghalandari. 2017. Revisiting the centroid-based method: A strong baseline for multi-document summarization. *arXiv preprint arXiv:1708.07690*.

Demian Gholipour Ghalandari and Georgiana Ifrim. 2020. Examining the state-of-the-art in news timeline summarization. *arXiv preprint arXiv:2005.10107*.

Jimmy Lin, Nitin Madnani, and Bonnie Dorr. 2010. Putting the user in the loop: interactive maximal marginal relevance for query-focused summarization. In *Human Language Technologies: The 2010 Annual Conference of the North American Chapter of the Association for Computational Linguistics*, pages 305–308.

Yan Liu, Sheng-hua Zhong, and Wenjie Li. 2012. Query-oriented multi-document summarization via unsupervised deep learning. In *Proceedings of the AAAI Conference on Artificial Intelligence*, volume 26.

Yinhan Liu, Myle Ott, Naman Goyal, Jingfei Du, Mandar Joshi, Danqi Chen, Omer Levy, Mike Lewis, Luke Zettlemoyer, and Veselin Stoyanov. 2019. Roberta: A robustly optimized bert pretraining approach. *arXiv preprint arXiv:1907.11692*.

Sebastian Martschat and Katja Markert. 2017. Improving rouge for timeline summarization. In *Proceedings of the 15th Conference of the European Chapter of the Association for Computational Linguistics: Volume 2, Short Papers*, pages 285–290.

Sebastian Martschat and Katja Markert. 2018. A temporally sensitive submodularity framework for timeline summarization. *arXiv preprint arXiv:1810.07949*.

Mohsen Mesgar, Edwin Simpson, Yue Wang, and Iryna Gurevych. 2020. Generating persona-consistent dialogue responses using deep reinforcement learning. *arXiv preprint arXiv:2005.00036*.

Volodymyr Mnih, Adria Puigdomenech Badia, Mehdi Mirza, Alex Graves, Timothy Lillicrap, Tim Harley, David Silver, and Koray Kavukcuoglu. 2016. Asynchronous methods for deep reinforcement learning. In *International conference on machine learning*, pages 1928–1937. PMLR.

Frederick Mosteller. 2006. Remarks on the method of paired comparisons: I. the least squares solution assuming equal standard deviations and equal correlations. In *Selected Papers of Frederick Mosteller*, pages 157–162. Springer.

Kiem-Hieu Nguyen, Xavier Tannier, and Véronique Moriceau. 2014. Ranking multidocument event descriptions for building thematic timelines. In *Proceedings of COLING 2014, the 25th International Conference on Computational Linguistics: Technical Papers*, pages 1208–1217.

Nils Reimers and Iryna Gurevych. 2019. Sentence-bert: Sentence embeddings using siamese bert-networks. *arXiv preprint arXiv:1908.10084*.

Cody Rioux, Sadid A Hasan, and Yllias Chali. 2014. Fear the reaper: A system for automatic multi-document summarization with reinforcement learning. In *Proceedings of the 2014 conference on empirical methods in natural language processing (EMNLP)*, pages 681–690.

Seonggi Ryang and Takeshi Abekawa. 2012. Framework of automatic text summarization using reinforcement learning. In *Proceedings of the 2012 Joint Conference on Empirical Methods in Natural Language Processing and Computational Natural Language Learning*, pages 256–265.

Edwin Simpson, Yang Gao, and Iryna Gurevych. 2020. Interactive text ranking with bayesian optimization: A case study on community qa and summarization. *Transactions of the Association for Computational Linguistics*, 8:759–775.

Haoyu Song, Wei-Nan Zhang, Jingwen Hu, and Ting Liu. 2020. Generating persona consistent dialogues by exploiting natural language inference. In *Proceedings of the AAAI Conference on Artificial Intelligence*, volume 34, pages 8878–8885.

Julius Steen and Katja Markert. 2019. Abstractive timeline summarization. In *Proceedings of the 2nd Workshop on New Frontiers in Summarization*, pages 21–31.

Jannik Strötgen and Michael Gertz. 2015. A baseline temporal tagger for all languages. In *Proceedings of the 2015 conference on empirical methods in natural language processing*, pages 541–547.

Louis L Thurstone. 1927. A law of comparative judgment. *Psychological review*, 34(4):273.

Giang Tran, Mohammad Alrifai, and Eelco Herder. 2015. Timeline summarization from relevant headlines. In *European Conference on Information Retrieval*, pages 245–256. Springer.

Giang Binh Tran, Tuan A Tran, Nam-Khanh Tran, Mohammad Alrifai, and Nattiya Kanhabua. 2013. Leveraging learning to rank in an optimization framework for timeline summarization. In *SIGIR 2013 Workshop on Time-aware Information Access (TAIA*.

Rui Yan, Xiaojun Wan, Jahna Otterbacher, Liang Kong, Xiaoming Li, and Yan Zhang. 2011. Evolutionary timeline summarization: a balanced optimization framework via iterative substitution. In *Proceedings of the 34th international ACM SIGIR conference on Research and development in Information Retrieval*, pages 745–754.

Jingqing Zhang, Yao Zhao, Mohammad Saleh, and Peter Liu. 2020. Pegasus: Pre-training with extracted gap-sentences for abstractive summarization. In *International Conference on Machine Learning*, pages 11328–11339. PMLR.

Dynamic Facet Selection by Maximizing Graded Relevance

Michael Glass * and **Md Faisal Mahbub Chowdhury** * and **Yu Deng** * and **Ruchi Mahindru** and **Nicolas Rodolfo Fauceglia** and **Alfio Gliozzo** and **Nandana Mihindukulasooriya**
IBM Research, T.J. Watson Research Center, Yorktown Heights, NY, USA
{mrglass, mchowdh, dengy, rmahindr, gliozzo}@us.ibm.com,
{nandana.m,nicolas.fauceglia,Gaetano.Rossiello}@ibm.com

Abstract

Dynamic faceted search (DFS), an interactive query refinement technique, is a form of Human–computer information retrieval (HCIR) approach. It allows users to narrow down search results through facets, where the facets-documents mapping is determined at runtime based on the context of user query instead of pre-indexing the facets statically. In this paper, we propose a new unsupervised approach for dynamic facet generation, namely *optimistic facets*, which attempts to generate the best possible subset of facets, hence maximizing expected Discounted Cumulative Gain (DCG), a measure of ranking quality that uses a graded relevance scale. We also release code to generate a new evaluation dataset. Through empirical results on two datasets, we show that the proposed DFS approach considerably improves the document ranking in the search results.

1 Introduction

Human–computer information retrieval (HCIR) is the study of techniques that takes advantage of human intelligence into the search process. Through a multi-step search process, it facilitates opportunities for human feedback by taking into account the query context. Examples of HCIR approaches include – faceted search, relevance feedback, automatic query reformulation, illustration by tag clouds, etc.

Faceted Search (FS) (Tunkelang, 2009), a form of HCIR, is a prevalent technique in e-commerce where document retrieval systems are augmented with faceted navigation. Facets are terms that present an overview on the variety of data available given the user query, thereby hinting at the most relevant refinement operations for zooming in on the target information need (Ben-yitzhak et al., 2008).

Traditional facet generation approaches present several drawbacks. Documents must be pre-tagged with an existing taxonomy, adding overhead in content curation and management. Moreover, such static facets lack contextual matching with documents or queries. Figure 1 shows an example of static/traditional facets.

Dynamic Faceted Search (DFS) overcomes such limitations (Dash et al., 2008). For **Dynamic facets**, the facet to document mapping is determined at run-time based on the context of user query instead of pre-indexing the facets statically. In other words, in an information retrieval (IR) system, there is no exclusive list of terms to be considered for dynamic facets and such facets are not known in advance. There is no pre-existing mapping of facets to the documents (that are indexed in the corresponding IR system). The mapping can only be created at the real-time when the query is submitted followed by generation of such facets based on the search results specific to the given query and are presented to the user along with the relevant documents.

In this paper, we present an approach for generating dynamic facets and selecting the best set of facets to be presented to the user. Hence, allowing the user to select relevant facets (if any) to interactively refine their queries, which in turn improves search results at each facet selection iteration. This interaction can be repeated until the user is satisfied with the results presented or no further refinement is possible.

Below we highlight the major contributions of our work –

- a new state-of-the-art unsupervised approach for dynamic facet generation (see Section 3) evaluated on two datasets (see Section 6), and
- a new benchmark dataset, `Stackoverflow-Technotes` (or,

* Equal contributions.

Proceedings of the First Workshop on Interactive Learning for Natural Language Processing , pages 32–39
August 5, 2021. ©2021 Association for Computational Linguistics

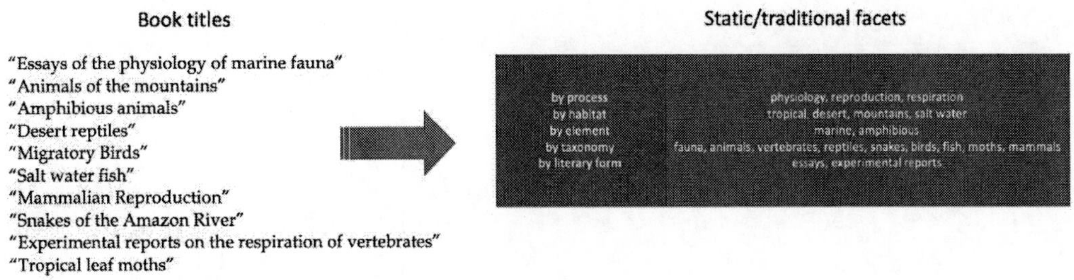

Figure 1: Example of static facets used to organize a set of book titles in a digital library.

simply `Stackoverflow`) Benchmark.[1] (see Section 5).

Rest of the paper is structured as follows. Section 2 includes a brief summary of related work with respect to DFS. Section 3 describes our proposed approaches. The next two sections (4 and 5) describes the experimental settings and datasets. In Section 6, we show the empirical results, both quantitative and qualitative. Finally, Section 7 concludes the paper and highlights perspectives for future work.

2 Related Work

A closely related research task of facet generation is to generate alternative queries, also known as query suggestion (Mei et al., 2008). Other related tasks are query substitution (Jones et al., 2006) and query refinement (Kraft and Zien, 2004). The main difference between these tasks and facet generation is that facets are not alternative/substitute/refined queries but rather a way to organize the search results obtained using the original query.

Another related task is query expansion (Xu and Croft, 1996) where the goal is adding related words to a query in order to increase the number of returned documents and improve recall accordingly. In contrast, selection of facets allow to narrow down search results.

There is a considerable amount of work on faceted search (Zheng et al., 2013; Kong, 2016). For brevity, here we focus on DFS only.

DFS can be divided into two categories. First, *DFS on databases* (Basu Roy et al., 2008; Kim et al., 2014; Vandic et al., 2018). Databases have a rich meta-data in the form of tables, attributes, dimensions, etc. DFS on databases focuses on the best possible attributes from the meta-data, to be presented as facets.

Our contributions are in the second category – *DFS on textual data*. An early approach was proposed by Ben-yitzhak et al. (2008), where the generated dynamic facets are constrained by the ability to sum pre-defined Boolean expressions. Dash et al. (2008) proposed an approach, given a keyword as query, to dynamically select a small set of "interesting" attributes and present their aggregation to a user. Their work is focused on evaluating the execution time rather than result re-ranking. Dakka and Ipeirotis (2008) proposed an approach using external resources, namely WordNet and Wikipedia, to generate facets given a query.

Our proposed DFS approach on text generates dynamic facets that are terms (which are not restricted), not just aggregated values, and does not rely on any external resource. Input queries can be natural language texts, not restricted to keywords.

In a recent relevant work, Mihindukulasooriya et al. (2020) proposed an unsupervised DFS approach that exploits different types of word embedding models to extract so called *flat* and *typed facets*. The *typed facets* are organized in hierarchies while the *flat facets* are simply a list of facets without hierarchy. They show empirically both set of facets yield similar results.

3 Proposed Dynamic Facet Generation

Given a ranked set of search results from a traditional search engine, our proposed approach, namely **Optimistic facet set selection**, tracks document ranking changes produced by selecting each candidate facet, and uses this information to select a subset of best possible facets.

We use the following notations in this section:

- $\mathbf{D} = [(d_1, s_1), (d_2, s_2), ..., (d_n, s_n)]$, where score $s_i \in \mathbb{R}$, is a list of n documents in search

[1] We provide the codes for automatically creating the dataset using publicly available data, and also to run the simulated automatic evaluation. They can be found here - `https://github.com/IBM/Stackoverflow-Technotes-dataset`.

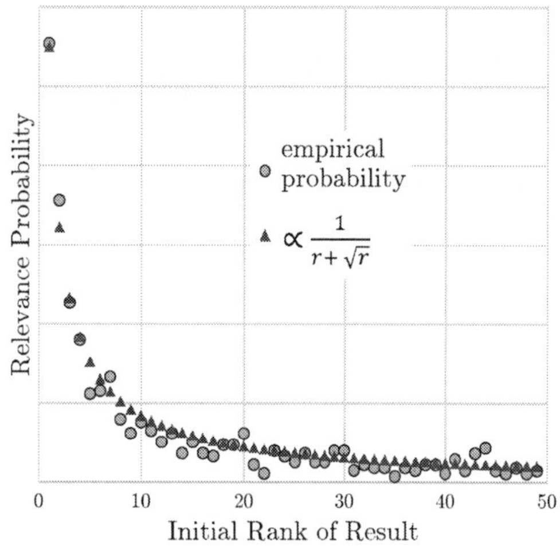

Figure 2: Relevance Probability

results for the initial query, q_0 returned by initial traditional IR component/search engine.

- $\mathcal{C} = \{f_1, f_2, ..., f_c\}$ is a set of c terms to be considered as facet candidates.
- $F \subset \mathcal{C}$ is a set of k facets generated by the system as output, where k can be set by the user or the interactive search system.

3.1 Facet candidate generation

Given a user query and the respective search results (i.e. documents) from a search engine, we extract the terms from those candidate documents with a frequency above threshold θ_{freq}. Let us limit the expected number of dynamic facets to k. Given a pre-trained word embedding model (for the indexed document collection), cosine similarity, $sim(q_0, t)$, between the query and each term t is computed. Up to the top c terms with a minimum similarity score of θ_{sim} are kept as **facet candidates.**[2]

3.2 Optimistic Facet Set Selection

Our algorithm is built on two key assumptions:

- ***Optimism***: the user will select the best facet: one that attains the best Discounted Cumulative Gain (DCG) (or other graded relevance measure).
- ***Relevance Probability***: how likely a document is to be relevant is approximated by its rank in initial search results.

[2]We set $\theta_{freq} = 3$, $\theta_{sim} = 0.5$, and $c = max(k^2, 50)$.

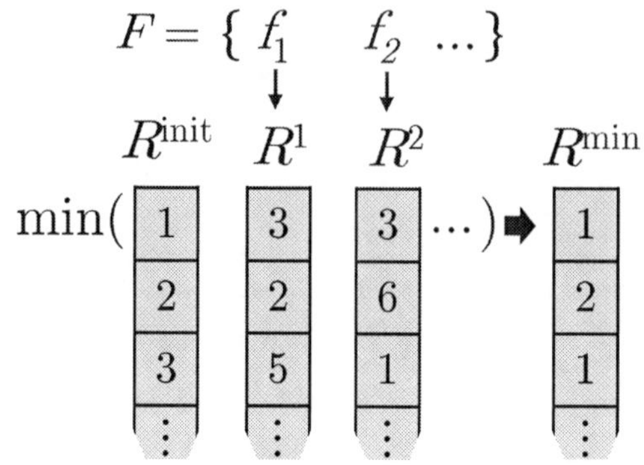

Figure 3: Minimum Rank (R^{min}) for Facet Set

Each candidate facet, f, is associated with some change in the scores of the document results, δ^f, and hence, some new ranking of the document results, R^f. Using the *filter* strategy, δ_i^f is set as $-\infty$ if f does not appear in document d_i, else zero. Experimenting with a strategy of computing the change in BM25 score (Robertson and Zaragoza, 2009) if f is added to the query, resulted in lower performance.

Suppose p_i is the probability of being relevant for the ith ranked document in the initial retrieval. We fit a curve to estimate p_i independent of the query or document results and find this probability to be roughly proportional to the inverse of the rank plus its square root. Figure 2 shows empirical probability of relevance and the curve to fit.

A facet set has a *minimum possible rank* for each document, the lowest rank that can be achieved by selecting any facet in the set, or no facet. We indicate this list of ranks as $R^{min} = [r_1, r_2, ..., r_n]$ where $r_j = \min\left(j, \min_{f \in F}(R_j^f)\right)$. The list of ranks R^{min} is closely connected with our optimistic assumption. If, for example, the single relevant document is in initial rank j, then R_j^{min} is the rank it will have after the user sees the initial results and optionally selects the best facet.

Consider the case (a majority in our datasets) where only one document is relevant. Then the expected DCG under the optimistic assumption is given by Equation 2. DCG is a standard metric in IR to measure the overall quality of the search results. DCG depends only on the ranks of the relevant ($rel_i = 1$) documents. Intuitively, we optimize DCG in expectation by providing facets that produce *different* and *likely* rankings for the returned documents.

$$DCG = \sum_{i=1}^{n} \frac{rel_i}{\log_2(1+i)} \quad (1)$$

$$\mathbb{E}(DCG_F) = \sum_{i=1}^{n} \frac{p_i}{\log_2(1+R_i^{min})} \quad (2)$$

We select a facet set to approximately optimize $\mathbb{E}(DCG_F)$ using greedy and local search. Both the greedy and local search phases of facet set selection rely on a function to select the facet candidate that will improve $\mathbb{E}(DCG_F)$ the most: $\texttt{Best}(\mathcal{C}, F, f^*, s^*)$. The greedy phase adds k facet candidates to the facet set, each time adding the facet that maximizes the set score. Local search tries to swap each facet in the facet set for some better facet candidate. This process could repeat until $\mathbb{E}(DCG_F)$ does not improve. Algorithm 1 shows pseudocode for these functions.

Algorithm 1 Greedy/Local Facet Set Selection

```
Best(C, F, f*, s*)                    Greedy(C, k)
  for f in C − F do                     F ← ∅
    s ← E(DCG_{F∪{f}})                  for i ← 1 through k do
    if s > s* then                        f*, s* ←Best(C, F, ∅, 0)
      f* ← f                              F ← F ∪ {f*}
      s* ← s                            end for
    end if                              return F, s*
  end for
  return f*, s*

LocalSearch(C, F, s*)

  repeat
    s0 ← s*
    for f0 in F do
      F ← F/f0
      f*, s* ← Best(C, F, f0, s*)
      F ← F ∪ {f*}
    end for
  until s* = s0
```

4 Experiments

Evaluation Settings: We use the simulated user based automatic evaluation, called ORACLE, proposed by Mihindukulasooriya et al. (2020). For each iteration of the faceted search, the system presents a list of ranked search results and facets to the ORACLE. It selects the facet which retrieves the target document at the highest rank.

5 Datasets

5.1 TechQA Benchmark

The first dataset is an existing benchmark of real-world user questions in English in the domain of technical customer support, named the TechQA dataset (Castelli et al., 2020). The reason we choose this dataset is - the most recent work, (Mihindukulasooriya et al., 2020)), that we are aware of for faceted search is evaluated on this dataset. The RoBERTa based state-of-the-art IR approach (Liu et al., 2019) that we use as one of the baselines also used this dataset. The TechQA dataset has **160** answerable questions in the Dev split and is aligned with a corpus of 801,998 publicly available IBM Technotes documents. We evaluate our approaches on these questions while treating the corresponding Technotes documents (containing the answers) as the corpus.

5.2 Proposed Stackoverflow Benchmark

In addition to the TechQA benchmark, we create a new dataset in the technical support domain to verify the generality of our approach. This allows us to evaluate it on a different benchmark containing real-world queries which are often noisy and not curated.

We are releasing the corresponding benchmark generation codes to the research community as part of this work. The dataset contains total **883** queries. It was created from Stackoverflow[3] forum threads. We only considered those queries where the accepted answer posts contain link(s) to documents in the Technotes corpus (the same corpus as mentioned in the TechQA Benchmark). Here is how the released codes create this new benchmark:

- **Extraction of Candidate Question Answer (QA) Pairs:** We first identify the set of question posts and corresponding accepted answer posts from the StackOverflow post history dump. Then we extract the *title* and *body* of the identified *question posts* from post history, considering that the post body further elaborates context of the question.
- **Validation of QA Pairs with Result Links:** We retain the QA pairs where desired corpus links have been mentioned in answer posts. This ensures that the questions in the dataset have answer links from the Technotes corpus.
- **Generation of Benchmark Dataset:** We then extract the Technotes IDs from the answer posts to form the benchmark dataset. Figure 4 shows an example of an entry in the dataset, which includes an *"id"* field containing the id of a question post, a *"title"* field about the title of the question post, a *"body"* field which is the body part of the question post, and a *"relevant_docids"*

[3]https://stackoverflow.com

field with a set of Technotes IDs extracted from the corresponding accepted answer post.

The procedure described above is generic and can be replicated for other forums and corpora with similar characteristics.

6 Results

We implemented the *flat facets* proposed by Mihindukulasooriya et al. (2020) to compare with our results on both datasets. We use BM25 (Robertson and Zaragoza, 2009) as IR baseline for the *Stackoverflow* benchmark. For the *TechQA* dataset, we use the state-of-the-art IR approach of Zhang et al. (2020) built using RoBERTa (Liu et al., 2019) as baseline. Zhang et al. (2020) generously shared with us their system's output for the *TechQA-DR* (i.e. document retrieval) task mentioned in their paper. We feed this output as input in our system as well as our implementation of Mihindukulasooriya et al. (2020) to extract facets from corresponding search results.

For a given query, we consider maximum 50 search results retrieved by the IR baseline. Then, the ORACLE accepts only up to 5 facets generated from a DFS approach, and chose only one facet (i.e. a single interaction with the DFS system) as a filter. If a corresponding search result does not containing this facet, it is discarded which changes ranks of some of the remaining search results.

6.1 Quantitative Evaluation

We use three standard evaluation metrics: *Discounted Cumulative Gain (DCG)*, *Mean Reciprocal Rank (MRR)*, and *Hits@K*. For *Hits@K*, we share the absolute number of queries where the expected document is ranked within top-K results.

Table 1 empirically compares our DFS approach against other systems. As evident from the results, *optimistic DFS* demonstrated remarkable edge over the DFS approach of Mihindukulasooriya et al. (2020) on both of the datasets in every single metric. Furthermore, our approach significantly improves the results of the underlying strong IR baselines in both datasets.

6.2 Qualitative Evaluation

For the qualitative evaluation, we selected a sample set of 22 random queries from the Stackoverflow dataset. We asked a Subject Matter Expert (SME), who is a customer support agent in the field, to manually inspect the facets (produced by *optimistic DFS*) for each selected query.

According to the SME, a facet is considered useful, if it is contextually related but not already mentioned in the user's (short) query (i.e. the 'title' in Figure 4) and either appears in (i) the fully specified query, aka 'post' (i.e. the 'body' in Figure 4), or (ii) in the target document.

Table 2 shows sample subset of *"User Query"*, their corresponding *"Top 5 Dynamically Generated Facets"*, *"Additional Relevant Facets Present in Post"* that the system could have considered to rank higher to place in the top 5, and *"SME Recommended Facets"* that the system should have presented (even though they are not seen in the post), as they are relevant for the corresponding user query. The values in the last two columns are provided by the SME.

The SME marked the dynamically generated facets into four following categories:

- "Facets seen in Post" (highlighted in *italic font*) – facets seen in the post body and our algorithm also generated e.g. *'ClearCase Remote Client (CCRC)'*;

- "Facets seen in Post and relevant for query" (highlighted in ***bold italic font***) – relevant facets seen in the post body and our algorithm also generated e.g ***'ClearCase Remote Client'***;

- "Facets unseen in Post" (highlighted in underline) – facets unseen in the post body that our algorithm also generated e.g. 'Rational ClearCase SCM Adapter', 'rad', 'source control';

- "Facets unseen in Post and relevant for query" (highlighted in **bold underline**) – relevant facets unseen in the post and our algorithm also generated e.g. **'dynamic views'**.

In summary, 22 randomly chosen queries and respective 5 facets per query generated from Optimistic DFS were evaluated by the SME. On average, our system generated 89% "Facets unseen in Post", out of which 25% are relevant for queries. Among the 11% "Facets seen in Post", 82% of them are found to be relevant for queries.

Metric	*TechQA* dataset				*Stackoverflow* dataset		
	RoBERTa baseline	*Zhang et al. (2020)*	*Flat DFS*	*Optimistic DFS*	*BM25*	*Flat DFS*	*Optimistic DFS*
DCG	0.76	0.82	0.84	**0.91**	0.18	0.24	**0.29**
MRR	0.69	0.77	0.80	**0.89**	0.13	0.20	**0.26**
Hits@1	92 (57.5%)	109 (68.1%)	116 (72.5%)	**138 (86.3%)**	75 (8.5%)	144 (16.3%)	**205 (23.2%)**
Hits@5	133 (83.1%)	141 (88.1%)	143 (89.4%)	**150 (93.8%)**	153 (17.3%)	228 (25.8%)	**260 (29.4%)**
Hits@10	137 (85.6%)	149 (93.1%)	151 (94.4%)	**153 (95.6%)**	200 (22.7%)	261 (29.6%)	**293 (33.2%)**

Table 1: DFS evaluation results using simulated user. *"Flat DFS"* refers to a DFS approach proposed by Mihindukulasooriya et al. (2020). *"RoBERTa baseline"* is the baseline for (our IR baseline) Zhang et al. (2020).

User Query	Top 5 Dynamically Generated Facets	Additional Relevant Facets Present in Post	Recommended Facets by SME
What are the differences between scm adapter and CCRC eclipse plugin?	**dynamic views**, rad, source control, Rational ClearCase SCM Adapter, ***ClearCase Remote Client***	Eclipse SCM adapter	CCRC plugin, ClearCase perspective, Eclipse workspace, ucm
CLEARCASE XPN not parsed as variable in clearcase command	**cleartool man**, cleartool mktrtype, command line, extended pathname, text file	linux	cleartool find
CCRC ClearCase Remote Client - Error 'Config spec for view. . . needs to be synchronized	*ClearCase Remote Client (CCRC)*, IBM Rational ClearCase Remote Client, **ucm**, *vob*, web view	synchronize with stream, CCRC Version: 7.1.1	
Unable to undo rebase stream	integration view, ***rebase operation***, recommended baseline, target view, **vob**		cleartool rebase
Web Service Auto Generated Files	WSDL file, **ear**, roundtrip, web services, xsd	SEI, ser, deser, helper files, BOUNTY EDIT	
What's the easiet way to detect "evil twins" in Rational ClearCase?	ClearCase MultiSite, IBM Rational ClearCase, ccrc, clearfsimport, **file element**	vob, ClearCase 7.1	cleartool, cleartool find
How to rename member baseline? Is it acceptable practice?	**new baseline**, project, pvob, rebase, rmbl	cleartool rmname, UCM, clearcase	lbtype, label type
Cleartool command: Get symlink path and target	***VOB symlink***, cleartool rmelem command, config spec, global path, **pathname**		

Table 2: Qualitative evaluation of *Optimistic DFS* output on the **Stackoverflow** dataset.

{
"id": "57357897",
"title": "Cannot locate webjars with SpringBoot application running on WebSphere",
"body": "I have been trying to host Spring Boot application on WebSphere server.\n\nVersions :\n\n - SpringBoot 2.1.6.RELEASE\n - WebSphere Liberty 19.0.0.6 with JavaEE 8\n - webjars-locator 0.36\n\nThe app was successfuly deployed on standalone Tomcat 9.0.22 and webjars could be resolved there. However for WebSphere I receive an error when trying to access webjars from `html` page ... ...",
"relevant_docids": [
"swg1PM99378"
]
}

Figure 4: Question Answer Pair Example

7 Conclusion

In this paper, we propose *Optimistic facet set selection*, a new unsupervised approach for dynamic facet generation for interactive search. It outperforms existing state of the art on two publicly available benchmarks, one of which we are releasing as part of this work.

We believe this new dataset will be useful for the research community for training and evaluating interactive models. Currently, our proposed approach does not have an active learning component and does not explicitly learn from the user feedback (e.g. fine-tuning an NLP model). However, we think our approach will serve as a strong baseline for the future interactive search approaches.

In future, we plan to investigate the following –

- how to leverage the proposed algorithm to generate facets automatically grouped by types.
- how dynamic facets can be generated using language models as Knowledge Bases.

Our vision is to transform the interactive search experience into a learnable knowledge discovery process.

References

Senjuti Basu Roy, Haidong Wang, Gautam Das, Ullas Nambiar, and Mukesh Mohania. 2008. Minimum-effort driven dynamic faceted search in structured databases. In *Proceedings of the International Conference on Information and Knowledge Management (CIKM 2008)*, pages 13–22.

Ori Ben-yitzhak, Nadav Golb, Nadav Har'el, Ronny Lempel, Andreas Neumann, Shila Ofek-koifman, Dafna Sheinwald, Eugene Shekita, Benjamin Sznajder, and Sivan Yogev. 2008. Beyond basic faceted search. In *Proceedings of the international conference on Web search and web data mining (WSDM 2008)*, pages 33–44.

Vittorio Castelli, Rishav Chakravarti, Saswati Dana, Anthony Ferritto, Radu Florian, Martin Franz, Dinesh Garg, Dinesh Khandelwal, Scott McCarley, Michael McCawley, Mohamed Nasr, Lin Pan, Cezar Pendus, John Pitrelli, Saurabh Pujar, Salim Roukos, Andrzej Sakrajda, Avi Sil, Rosario Uceda-Sosa, Todd Ward, and Rong Zhang. 2020. The TechQA dataset. In *Proceedings of the 58th Annual Meeting of the Association for Computational Linguistics*, pages 1269–1278, Online. Association for Computational Linguistics.

Wisam Dakka and Panos Ipeirotis. 2008. Automatic Extraction of Useful Facet Hierarchies from Text Databases. In *Proceedings of the IEEE 24th International Conference on Data Engineering (ICDE 2008)*, pages 466 – 475.

Debabrata Dash, Jun Rao, Nimrod Megiddo, Anastasia Ailamaki, and Guy M. Lohman. 2008. Dynamic Faceted Search for Discovery-driven Analysis. In *Proceedings of the International Conference on Information and Knowledge Management (CIKM 2008)*, pages 3–12.

Rosie Jones, Benjamin Rey, Omid Madani, and Wiley Greiner. 2006. Generating query substitutions. In *Proceedings of the 15th International Conference on World Wide Web (WWW '06)*.

Hak-Jin Kim, Yongjun Zhu, Wooju Kim, and Taimao Sun. 2014. Dynamic faceted navigation in decision making using semantic web technology. In *Decision Support Systems*, volume 61, pages 59 – 68.

Weize Kong. 2016. *Extending Faceted Search to the Open-Domain Web*. Ph.D. thesis, College of Information and Computer Sciences, University of Massachusetts Amherst, MA, USA.

Reiner Kraft and Jason Zien. 2004. Mining anchor text for query refinement. In *Proceedings of the 13th International Conference on World Wide Web (WWW '04)*.

Yinhan Liu, Myle Ott, Naman Goyal, Jingfei Du, Mandar Joshi, Danqi Chen, Omer Levy, Mike Lewis, Luke Zettlemoyer, and Veselin Stoyanov. 2019. Roberta: A robustly optimized bert pretraining approach. *arXiv preprint arXiv:1907.11692*.

Qiaozhu Mei, Dengyong Zhou, and Kenneth Church. 2008. Query suggestion using hitting time. In *Proceedings of the 17th ACM conference on Information and knowledge management (CIKM '08)*.

Nandana Mihindukulasooriya, Ruchi Mahindru, Md Faisal Mahbub Chowdhury, Yu Deng, Nicolas Rodolfo Fauceglia, Gaetano Rossiello, Sarthak Dash, Alfio Gliozzo, and Shu Tao. 2020. Dynamic faceted search for technical support exploiting induced knowledge. In *International Semantic Web Conference*, pages 683–699. Springer, Cham.

Stephen Robertson and Hugo Zaragoza. 2009. The probabilistic relevance framework: Bm25 and beyond. *Foundations and Trends in Information Retrieval*, 3:333–389.

Daniel Tunkelang. 2009. Faceted Search. In *Synthesis Lectures on Information Concepts, Retrieval, and Services*, volume 1, pages 1–80. Morgan & Claypool Publishers.

Damir Vandic, Steven S. Aanen, Flavius Frasincar, and Uzay Kaymak. 2018. Dynamic Facet Ordering for Faceted Product Search Engines. In *IEEE Transactions on Knowledge and Data Engineering*, volume 29, pages 1004 – 1016.

Jinxi Xu and W. Bruce Croft. 1996. Query expansion using local and global document analysis. In *Proceedings of the 19th Annual International ACM SIGIR Conference on Research and Development in Information Retrieval (SIGIR '96)*.

Rong Zhang, Revanth Gangi Reddy, Md Arafat Sultan, Vittorio Castelli, Anthony Ferritto, Radu Florian, Efsun Sarioglu Kayi, Salim Roukos, Avi Sil, and Todd Ward. 2020. Multi-stage pre-training for low-resource domain adaptation. In *Proceedings of the 2020 Conference on Empirical Methods in Natural Language Processing (EMNLP)*, pages 5461–5468, Online. Association for Computational Linguistics.

Bweijunl Zheng, Wei Zhang, and Xiaoyu Fu Boqin Feng. 2013. A survey of faceted search. *Journal of Web engineering*, 12(1&2):041–064.

Active Curriculum Learning

Borna Jafarpour[1], **Nicolai Pogrebnyakov**[1,2], **Dawn Sepehr**[1]
[1] Thomson Reuters, Toronto, Canada
[2] Copenhagen Business School, Frederiksberg, Denmark
{firstname.lastname}@thomsonreuters.com

Abstract

This paper investigates and reveals the relationship between two closely related machine learning disciplines, namely Active Learning (AL) and Curriculum Learning (CL), from the lens of several novel curricula. This paper also introduces Active Curriculum Learning (ACL) which improves AL by combining AL with CL to benefit from the dynamic nature of the AL informativeness concept as well as the human insights used in the design of the curriculum heuristics. Comparison of the performance of ACL and AL on two public datasets for the Named Entity Recognition (NER) task shows the effectiveness of combining AL and CL using our proposed framework.

1 Introduction

Modern deep learning architectures predominantly need large amounts of labeled data to achieve high levels of performance. In the presence of a large unlabeled corpus, data points are usually chosen randomly to be annotated. However, annotation can be a costly task and not all the annotations are equally beneficial. Active Learning (AL) aims to reduce the number of annotations required to train a machine learning model by choosing the most "informative" unlabeled data for annotation. The informativeness is determined by querying a model or a set of models trained on the available annotated data (Settles 2012). Algorithm 1 shows AL more formally.

Several categories of informativeness score have been developed in the literature. For example, uncertainty metrics select unlabeled data for which the model has the highest uncertainty of label prediction (Settles and Craven 2008). Examples of uncertainty measures for a classification task are the difference of the probability of prediction for the first and second most likely classes (i.e., the margin of the prediction probability) and the entropy of prediction over all classes (i.e., $-\sum_{i=1}^{c} p_i \log p_i$ where c is the number of classes). Lower values of margin and higher values of entropy metrics are associated with higher uncertainty and consequently informativeness. Some other examples of informativeness scoring methods for unlabeled data are the amount of prediction disagreement in a committee of models (Melville and Mooney 2004) and the amount of expected change to model weights (Zhang, Lease, and Wallace 2017) or loss value (Long et al. 2014).

Curriculum Learning (CL), on the other hand, attempts to mimic how humans learn and uses that knowledge to train better models (Bengio et al. 2009; Soviany et al. 2021). Complex topics are taught to humans based on a curriculum which takes into account the level of difficulty of the material presented to the learner. CL borrows this idea and engages the human experts to design a metric that is used to sort the annotated training data from "easy" to "hard" to be presented to the model during training (Bengio et al. 2009). The

1. Seed labeled data $\boldsymbol{D^L} = \{(x_1, y_1), \ldots, (x_k, y_k)\}$
2. Unlabeled data $\boldsymbol{D^U} = \{x_{k+1}, \ldots, x_m\}$
3. While the stopping criterion is not met:
   3.1. Fine-tune or train model $\boldsymbol{M}$ on $\boldsymbol{D^L}$
   3.2. $\boldsymbol{I} :=$ the set of i most informative data samples in $\boldsymbol{D^U}$ according to $\boldsymbol{M}$
   3.3. $\boldsymbol{D^U} := \boldsymbol{D^U} \setminus \boldsymbol{I}$; $\boldsymbol{D^L} := \boldsymbol{D^L} \cup \boldsymbol{L(I)}$

Algorithm 1: Steps of the AL algorithm where $L(\boldsymbol{I})$ denotes the set $\boldsymbol{I}$ after annotation. An example of stopping criterion can be a minimum value for accuracy.

1. Training data $\boldsymbol{D^T} = \{\}$
2. Available data $\boldsymbol{D^A} = \{(x_1, y_1), \ldots, (x_n, y_n)\}$
3. Repeat until $\boldsymbol{D^A}$ is empty:
   3.1. $\boldsymbol{I} :=$ the set of $\boldsymbol{k}$ easiest examples in $\boldsymbol{D^A}$ according to *a fixed curriculum*
   3.2. $\boldsymbol{D^T} := \boldsymbol{D^T} \cup \boldsymbol{I}$; $\boldsymbol{D^A} := \boldsymbol{D^A} \setminus \boldsymbol{I}$
   3.3. Fine-tune existing model $\boldsymbol{M}$ on $\boldsymbol{D^T}$

Algorithm 2: Steps of the CL algorithm.

Proceedings of the First Workshop on Interactive Learning for Natural Language Processing , pages 40–45
August 5, 2021. ©2021 Association for Computational Linguistics

goal of CL is to find a better local optimum faster compared to randomly presenting the data to the model by smoothing the loss function in early stages of training. CL algorithm is presented in Algorithm 2. CL has been investigated in computer vision (Gui, Baltrusaitis, and Morency 2017), Natural Language Processing (NLP) (Rao, Anuranjana, and Mamidi 2020), and speech recognition (Braun, Neil, and Liu 2016) among others (Soviany et al. 2021). Specifically within NLP, CL has been used on tasks such as question answering (Sachan and Xing 2016), natural language understanding (Xu et al. 2020), as well as learning word representations (Tsvetkov et al. 2016). Different curriculum designs has been investigated by considering heuristics such as sentence length, word frequency, language model score, and parse tree depth (Tsvetkov et al. 2016; Platanios et al. 2019).

Other related approaches such as self-paced learning (SPL) (Kumar, Packer, and Koller 2010) and self-paced curriculum learning (Jiang et al. 2015) have also been proposed to show the efficacy of a designed curriculum which adapts dynamically to the pace at which the learner progresses. Other attempts at improving an AL strategy include self-paced active learning (Tang and Huang 2019) in which the authors introduce practical techniques to consider informativeness, representativeness, and easiness of samples while querying for labels. Such methods that only focus on designing a curriculum miss, in general, the opportunity to also leverage the ability of the predictive model which progresses as new labeled data becomes available.

The addition of CL injects human expertise into learning manifested in the design of a curriculum. This is in contrast with previous studies that combined AL with SPL (Tang and Huang 2019; Lin et al. 2018). SPL is inspired by CL but, similarly to AL, relies on querying the model being trained to select instances for labeling.

Our contributions in this paper are twofold: (i) we shed light on the relationship between AL and CL by investigating if AL enforces (or follows) a curriculum. To this end, we monitor and visualize a variety of novel curricula during the AL simulation loop; (ii) We propose a novel method which we call Active Curriculum Learning (ACL). ACL takes advantage of the benefits of both CL (i.e., designing a curriculum for the model to follow) and AL (i.e., choosing samples based on the enhanced ability of the predictive model) at the same time to improve AL. Our preliminary experiments show that the performance of an AL strategy will be improved by deliberately combining AL and CL concepts. This article presents the foundation of this method accompanied by the preliminary results and in our future work we will explore its effectiveness more extensively by implementing more experiments and performing hyper parameter tuning as well as exploring other NLP tasks beyond NER.

2 Novel Curricula

Other than the most explored curriculum features such as sentence length and word frequency some other curricula for measuring diversity, simplicity, and prototypicality of the samples are proposed in (Tsvetkov et al. 2016). Our conjecture is that large-scale language models and also linguistic features can be used to design NLP curricula. We design seven novel curricula which assign a score to a sentence indicating its level of difficulty for a specific NLP task. Then, to acquire a curriculum, sentences are sorted by their corresponding scores. Other than our 7 novel curricula, we also experiment with the following commonly used curricula:

1. **SENT_LEN:** Number of words in a sentence.
2. **WORD_FREQ:** Average of frequency of the words in a sentence (e.g., frequency of the word A is calculated by $\frac{N_A}{\sum_{w \in V} N_w}$ where V is the set of the unique vocabulary of the labeled dataset, and N_w is the number of times the word w has appeared in the labeled dataset).

Our seven novel curricula are as follows:

1. **PARSE_CHILD:** Average of the number of children of words in the sentence parse tree.
2. **GPT_SCORE:** Sentence score according to the GPT2 language model (Radford et al. 2019) calculated as follows: $\sum_k \log(p(w_k))$ where $p(w_k)$ is the probability of kth word of the sentence according to the GPT2 model.
3. **LL_LOSS:** Average loss of the words in a sentence from the Longformer language model (Beltagy, Peters, and Cohan 2020)

For the following four novel curricula, we use the spaCy library (Honnibal and Montani 2017) to replace a word in a sentence with one of its linguistic features. The curriculum value for a sentence is then calculated exactly in the same way as word frequency but with one of the linguistic features instead of the word itself:

4. **POS**: Simple universal part-of-speech tag such as *PROPN*, *AUX* or *VERB*.
5. **TAG**: Detailed part-of-speech tag such as *NNP*, *VBZ*, *VBG*.
6. **SHAPE**: Shape of the word. For example, shapes of "Apple" and "12a." are "Xxxxx" and "ddx." respectively.
7. **DEP**: Syntactic relation connecting the word to its parent in the dependency parse tree of the sentence (e.g., *amod*, and *compound)*.

3 The Relationship between AL and CL and the Experimental Setup

We set out to answer the following question: *what is the relationship between AL and CL from the lens of the nine curricula?* To answer this question, we simulate two AL strategies as well as random strategy and monitor the curriculum metrics on the most informative samples (from the unlabeled data) chosen for annotation by each sampling strategy and compare them. We use the following two informativeness measures for unlabeled sentences in our AL strategies: (i) min-margin: minimum of margin of the prediction probability for the sentence tokens is considered as the AL score for that sentence. Sentences with lower scores are preferred, (ii) max-entropy: maximum of entropy of the prediction probability for the sentence tokens are considered as the AL score for that sentence and sentences with higher scores are preferred.

For the experiments, we use a single layer Bi-LSTM model (Lample et al. 2016) with the hidden state size of 768, enhanced with a 2-layer feed-forward network in which the number of hidden and output layers' nodes are equal to the number of classes in the dataset. The input to the LSTM model is the word2vec embedding (Mikolov et al. 2013) of sentence words. We use ADAM optimizer (Kingma and Ba 2017) with the batch size of 64 and the learning rate of 5e-4. We experiment with two publicly available English-language NER datasets: *OntoNotes5*[1], and *CoNLL 2003*[2] and use early stopping on the loss of the provided validation sets. Furthermore, we start with 500 randomly selected sentences as the seed data and

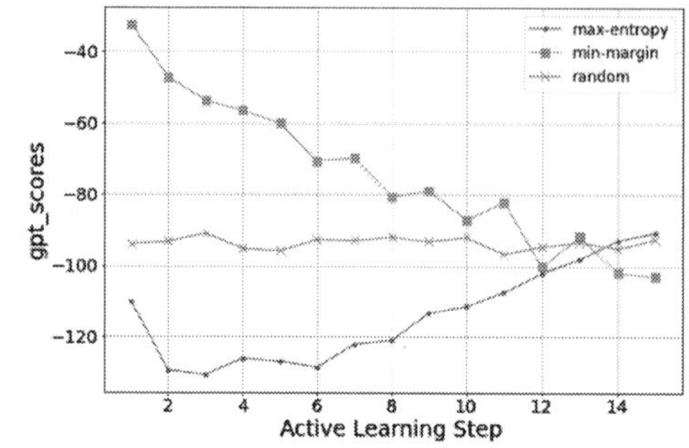

Figure 1: Comparison of the mean of GPT score of sentences added to training data in each iteration between random, min-margin and max-entropy AL strategies for the CoNLL dataset (average of 3 runs).

choose 500 sentences to be labeled in each iteration for a total of 15 iterations.

Figure 1 illustrates the experimental results of monitoring GPT score during AL loop. This figure clearly shows that GPT score of sentences chosen by max-entropy tends to have lower values (i.e., more complex sentences) and min-margin tends to choose sentences with higher values (i.e., simpler sentences) compared to a random strategy. Similar figures for other curricula reveal peculiarities of the different AL strategies compared to the random strategy and other AL strategies. Due to space limitations, instead of including such figures for different strategies, we calculate the following metric which we call Mean Normalized Difference (MND) to quantify how an AL selection strategy differs from a random strategy in choosing the most informative unlabeled data based on a curriculum. This metric is defined as follows:

$$MND = \sum_{i=1}^{n} \sum_{j=1}^{k} \frac{N\left(\psi^{CL}(RN_{ij})\right) - N\left(\psi^{CL}(AL_{ij})\right)}{n \times k} \quad (1)$$

where n is the number of iterations where we add k newly labeled sentences to the labeled dataset, ψ^{CL} calculates the value of the curriculum feature for a sentence, RN_{ij} and AL_{ij} are the jth sentence out of k chosen for annotation in the ith step of the random and active strategies, respectively, $N(x) := \frac{x - r_{min}^{CL}}{r_{max}^{CL} - r_{min}^{CL}}$, $r_{min}^{CL} := \min_{i \in [1,n]} \frac{\sum_{j=1}^{k} \psi^{CL}(R_{ij})}{k}$, and $r_{max}^{CL} := \max_{i \in [1,n]} \sum_{j=1}^{k} \frac{\psi^{CL}(R_{ij})}{k}$. In theory, the MND score can take any value. If the MND score of an AL strategy for a curriculum is close to zero, it means the curriculum values (ψ^{CL}) of the data chosen for

[1] Available at https://catalog.ldc.upenn.edu/LDC2013T19

[2] Available at https://www.clips.uantwerpen.be/conll2003/ner/

annotation are close to that of the random strategy. This, however, does not imply that the same unlabeled data is chosen by the two techniques. Furthermore, large values of the MND score indicate that AL chooses unlabeled data for annotation that have different curriculum scores compared to the random strategy. Since MND is normalized, we can compare the MND score of any two combinations of AL strategy and curriculum score to compare the degree to which they diverge from random strategy.

Experimental Results: Results of the MND scores for different curriculum features on the two experimental datasets are reported in Table 1. In most of these experiments, we observe that there is a difference between how random strategy and AL choose unlabeled dataset from the lens of MND as if AL is mimicking curriculum learning. We also observe that not all AL strategies consistently have the same MND sign for a curriculum on OntoNotes5 and CoNLL 2003 datasets but a noticeable divergence from the random strategy is evident. Table 1 also shows that the largest difference between active and random strategies in following curricula in our experiments is DEP/Min-Margin combination and the smallest difference between them is POS/Max-Entropy combination, both for OntoNotes5 dataset.

	CoNLL 2003		OntoNotes5	
	Min-Margin	Max-Entropy	Min-Margin	Max-Entropy
DEP	-16.7	2	-66.3	-5.5
POS	-18.2	-0.1	-4.2	-5.9
SHAPE	4.1	-3	12.5	4.7
TAG	-14.3	0.3	-4.3	-8.7
GPT_SCORE	-3.3	3.5	-9.0	6.3
LL_LOSS	-1.5	1.1	-18.1	1.7
PARSE_CHILD	3.1	-1.7	18.1	-0.9
SENT_LEN	4.7	-3.9	10.7	-6.2
WORD_FREQ	1.9	-2.4	-0.7	-0.1

Table 1: Mean Normalized Difference of min-margin and max-entropy for the two datasets CoNLL 2003 and OntoNotes5 (average of 15 steps and 3 runs).

4 Active Curriculum Learning (ACL)

To improve the performance of the AL strategies, we introduce a simple yet effective method leveraging both advantages of AL and CL which we call Active Curriculum Learning (ACL). The goal of this proposed method is to benefit from the dynamic nature of AL data selection metric while utilizing experts' knowledge in designing a fixed curriculum. To this end, in each step of the ACL loop, we use the following linear combination of the AL and CL scores to choose the most informative unlabeled data:

$$\psi^{ACL}(s, M_i) := \alpha \frac{\psi^{CL}(s)}{\max_{s\in D_i^U} |\psi^{CL}(s)|} + \beta \frac{\psi^{AL}(s, M_i)}{\max_{s\in D_i^U} |\psi^{AL}(s, M_i)|} \quad (2)$$

where D_i^U is the set of unlabeled sentences in step i of the ACL loop, α and β are the two parameters that control the combination of AL and CL scores, $\psi^{AL}(s, M_i)$ is the AL score (i.e., informativeness) of sentence s according to the predictive model M_i trained on D_i^L at step i.

The overall steps of the ACL algorithm are presented in Algorithm 3. Similar to the AL algorithm, the min-margin based strategy favors sentences with lower ψ^{ACL} for annotation and the opposite is true for the max-entropy based approach.

1. Seed labeled data $D^L = \{(x_1, y_1), \ldots, (x_m, y_m)\}$
2. Unlabeled data $D^U = \{x_{m+1}, \ldots, x_n\}$
3. While the stopping criterion is not met:
   3.1. $I :=$ the set of k examples in D^U with the best score based on ψ^{ACL}}
   3.2. $D^U := D^U \setminus I$; $D^L := D^L \cup L(I)$
   3.3. Fine-tune or train the model M_i on D^L

Algorithm 3. Steps of the ACL algorithm where $L(I)$ denotes the set I after annotation.

Experimental Results: We use the training setup of section 3 and perform token classification on CoNLL 2003 and OntoNotes5 datasets using the ACL algorithm. To evaluate the performance of ACL, for each AL metric and dataset combination, we run 18 ACL experiments where $\alpha = 1, \beta = 0.5$ or $\beta = -0.5$ for the 9 curricula, and also one AL experiment where $\alpha = 1$ and $\beta = 0$. Since the main focus of this article is to demonstrate if the introduction of a curriculum adds value to the performance of the active strategies, we select these hyper parameters in such a way that the effects of the active strategies are still dominant in the proposed model.

In each step of the ACL loop, we measure the token-level F1 score (for higher granularity) of the provided test set using the trained model in that step. Table 2 reports the average of F1 scores for the top 5 ACL combinations as well as the active learner ($\alpha = 1, \beta = 0$) across all runs (3) and steps (15). In all of our experiments, the top 5 ACL

OntoNotes5					
Min-Margin			Max-Entropy		
CM	**β**	**F1**	**CM**	**β**	**F1**
GPT_SCORE	0.5	0.4	LL_LOSS	-0.5	0.48
PARSE_CHILD	-0.5	0.4	DEP	-0.5	0.45
SENT_LEN	-0.5	0.38	POS	-0.5	0.43
LL_LOSS	0.5	0.37	WORD_FREQ	-0.5	0.43
TAG	-0.5	0.33	SENT_LEN	-0.5	0.43
-	0	0.23	-	0	0.36
CoNLL 2003					
Min-Margin			Max-Entropy		
CM	**β**	**F1**	**CM**	**β**	**F1**
LL_LOSS	0.5	0.65	SENT_LEN	0.5	0.67
GPT_SCORE	0.5	0.63	LL_LOSS	0.5	0.66
PARSE_CHILD	-0.5	0.63	WORD_FREQ	-0.5	0.66
SENT_LEN	-0.5	0.62	PARSE_CHILD	0.5	0.66
DEP	0.5	0.61	GPT_SCORE	-0.5	0.66
-	0	0.57	-	0	0.64

Table 2: ACL results for OntoNotes5 and CoNLL datasets. The last row for each experiment corresponds to the AL strategy. Curriculum Metric is denoted by CM, F1 is the average of F1 score across all 15 steps and 3 runs. For all experiments we have $\alpha = 1$.

combinations always outperformed AL for that dataset. In particular our curricula based on deep language models (GPT_SCORE and LL_LOSS) are appearing frequently in Table 2 indicating their utility.

5 Conclusions and Future Work

To the best of our knowledge, this is the first work to investigate and reveal the relationship between two closely related machine learning techniques namely, AL and CL. We observed that AL in fact follows a curriculum as it progresses through its iterations compared to the random strategy.

This is also the first work to take advantage of the benefits of both CL (i.e., designing a curriculum for the model to learn) and AL (i.e., choosing samples based on the improved ability of the predictive model) to improve AL in a unified model.

In our future work, we are interested in understanding in detail how CL helps AL, and exploring model-based techniques of combining AL and CL rather than a fixed set of weights for α and β. Another interesting question to investigate is to conduct similar experiments for other NLP tasks or using multiple curricula together with AL can be beneficial in reducing the annotation cost. We are also interested in investigating our novel curricula on their own in an isolated CL setting.

References

Beltagy, Iz, Matthew E. Peters, and Arman Cohan. 2020. "Longformer: The Long-Document Transformer." *ArXiv:2004.05150 [Cs]*, December. http://arxiv.org/abs/2004.05150.

Bengio, Yoshua, Jerome Louradour, Ronan Collobert, and Jason Weston. 2009. "Curriculum Learning." In *Proceedings of the 26th Annual International Conference on Machine Learning*, 41–48. Https://Doi.Org/10.1145/1553374.1553380. Montreal, Quebec, Canada: Association for Computing Machinery. https://doi.org/10.1145/1553374.1553380.

Braun, Stefan, Daniel Neil, and Shih-Chii Liu. 2016. "A Curriculum Learning Method for Improved Noise Robustness in Automatic Speech Recognition." *ArXiv:1606.06864 [Cs]*, September. http://arxiv.org/abs/1606.06864.

Gui, Liangke, Tadas Baltrusaitis, and Louis-Philippe Morency. 2017. "Curriculum Learning for Facial Expression Recognition." In *2017 12th IEEE International Conference on Automatic Face & Gesture Recognition (FG 2017)*, 505–11. Washington, DC, DC, USA: IEEE. https://doi.org/10.1109/FG.2017.68.

Honnibal, Matthew, and Ines Montani. 2017. "SpaCy 2: Natural Language Understanding with Bloom Embeddings, Convolutional Neural Networks and Incremental Parsing."

Jiang, Lu, Deyu Meng, Qian Zhao, Shiguang Shan, and Alexander G. Hauptmann. 2015. "Self-Paced Curriculum Learning." In *Proceedings of the Twenty-Ninth AAAI Conference on Artificial Intelligence*, 2694–2700. AAAI'15. Austin, Texas: AAAI Press.

Kingma, Diederik P., and Jimmy Ba. 2017. "Adam: A Method for Stochastic Optimization." *ArXiv:1412.6980 [Cs]*, January. http://arxiv.org/abs/1412.6980.

Kumar, M., Benjamin Packer, and Daphne Koller. 2010. "Self-Paced Learning for Latent Variable Models." In *Advances in Neural Information Processing Systems*. Vol. 23. Curran Associates, Inc. https://proceedings.neurips.cc/paper/2010/file/e57c6b956a6521b28495f2886ca0977a-Paper.pdf.

Lample, Guillaume, Miguel Ballesteros, Sandeep Subramanian, Kazuya Kawakami, and Chris Dyer. 2016. "Neural Architectures for Named Entity Recognition." In *Proceedings of the 2016 Conference of the North American Chapter of the Association for Computational Linguistics: Human Language Technologies*, 260–70. San Diego, California: Association for Computational Linguistics. https://doi.org/10.18653/v1/N16-1030.

Lin, Liang, Keze Wang, Deyu Meng, Wangmeng Zuo, and Lei Zhang. 2018. "Active Self-Paced Learning for Cost-Effective and Progressive Face Identification." *IEEE Transactions on Pattern*

Analysis and Machine Intelligence 40 (1): 7–19. https://doi.org/10.1109/TPAMI.2017.2652459.

Long, Bo, Jiang Bian, Olivier Chapelle, Ya Zhang, Yoshiyuki Inagaki, and Yi Chang. 2014. "Active Learning for Ranking through Expected Loss Optimization." *IEEE Transactions on Knowledge and Data Engineering* 27 (5): 1180–91.

Melville, Prem, and Raymond J. Mooney. 2004. "Diverse Ensembles for Active Learning." In *Twenty-First International Conference on Machine Learning - ICML '04*, 74. Banff, Alberta, Canada: ACM Press. https://doi.org/10.1145/1015330.1015385.

Mikolov, Tomas, Kai Chen, Greg Corrado, and Jeffrey Dean. 2013. "Efficient Estimation of Word Representations in Vector Space." *ArXiv Preprint ArXiv:1301.3781*.

Platanios, Emmanouil Antonios, Otilia Stretcu, Graham Neubig, Barnabas Poczos, and Tom Mitchell. 2019. "Competence-Based Curriculum Learning for Neural Machine Translation." In *Proceedings of the 2019 Conference of the North {A}merican Chapter of the Association for Computational Linguistics: Human Language Technologies, Volume 1 (Long and Short Papers)*, 1162–117. Minneapolis, Minnesota: Association for Computational Linguistics. https://doi.org/10.18653/v1/N19-1119.

Radford, Alec, Jeffrey Wu, Rewon Child, David Luan, Dario Amodei, and Ilya Sutskever. 2019. "Language Models Are Unsupervised Multitask Learners." *Ilya* (blog). 2019.

Rao, Vijjini Anvesh, Kaveri Anuranjana, and Radhika Mamidi. 2020. "A Sentiwordnet Strategy for Curriculum Learning in Sentiment Analysis." In *Natural Language Processing and Information Systems*, edited by Elisabeth Métais, Farid Meziane, Helmut Horacek, and Philipp Cimiano, 12089:170–78. Lecture Notes in Computer Science. Cham: Springer International Publishing. https://doi.org/10.1007/978-3-030-51310-8_16.

Sachan, Mrinmaya, and Eric Xing. 2016. "Easy Questions First? A Case Study on Curriculum Learning for Question Answering." In *Proceedings of the 54th Annual Meeting of the Association for Computational Linguistics (Volume 1: Long Papers)*, 453–63. Association for Computational Linguistics. https://doi.org/10.18653/v1/P16-1043.

Settles, Burr. 2012. "Active Learning." *Synthesis Lectures on Artificial Intelligence and Machine Learning* 6 (1): 1–114.

Settles, Burr, and Mark Craven. 2008. "An Analysis of Active Learning Strategies for Sequence Labeling Tasks." In *Proceedings of the Conference on Empirical Methods in Natural Language Processing - EMNLP '08*, 1070. Honolulu, Hawaii: Association for Computational Linguistics. https://doi.org/10.3115/1613715.1613855.

Soviany, Petru, Radu Tudor Ionescu, Paolo Rota, and Nicu Sebe. 2021. "Curriculum Learning: A Survey." *ArXiv:2101.10382 [Cs]*, January. http://arxiv.org/abs/2101.10382.

Tang, Ying-Peng, and Sheng-Jun Huang. 2019. "Self-Paced Active Learning: Query the Right Thing at the Right Time." In *Proceedings of the AAAI Conference on Artificial Intelligence*, 5117–24. https://doi.org/10.1609/aaai.v33i01.33015117.

Tsvetkov, Yulia, Manaal Faruqui, Wang Ling, Brian MacWhinney, and Chris Dyer. 2016. "Learning the Curriculum with Bayesian Optimization for Task-Specific Word Representation Learning." In *Proceedings of the 54th Annual Meeting of the Association for Computational Linguistics (Volume 1: Long Papers)*, 130–39. Association for Computational Linguistics. https://doi.org/10.18653/v1/P16-1013.

Xu, Benfeng, Licheng Zhang, Zhendong Mao, Quan Wang, Hongtao Xie, and Yongdong Zhang. 2020. "Curriculum Learning for Natural Language Understanding." In *Proceedings of the 58th Annual Meeting of the Association for Computational Linguistics*, 6095–6104. Association for Computational Linguistics. https://doi.org/10.18653/v1/2020.acl-main.542.

Zhang, Ye, Matthew Lease, and Byron C. Wallace. 2017. "Active Discriminative Text Representation Learning." In *Proceedings of the Thirty-First AAAI Conference on Artificial Intelligence*, 3386–92. AAAI'17. AAAI Press.

Tackling Fake News Detection by Interactively Learning Representations using Graph Neural Networks

Nikhil Mehta
Department of Computer Science
Purdue University, West Lafayette, IN
mehta52@purdue.edu

Dan Goldwasser
Department of Computer Science
Purdue University, West Lafayette, IN
dgoldwas@purdue.edu

Abstract

Easy access, variety of content, and fast widespread interactions are some of the reasons that have made social media increasingly popular in today's society. However, this has also enabled the widespread propagation of fake news, text that is published with an intent to spread misinformation and sway beliefs. Detecting fake news is important to prevent misinformation and maintain a healthy society.

While prior works have tackled this problem by building supervised learning systems, automatedly modeling the social media landscape that enables the spread of fake news is challenging. On the contrary, having humans fact check all news is not scalable. Thus, in this paper, we propose to approach this problem *interactively*, where human insight can be continually combined with an automated system, enabling better social media representation quality. Our experiments show performance improvements in this setting.

1 Introduction

Over the last decade, an increasing number of people access news online (Amy Mitchell, 2016), often using social networking platforms to engage, consume and propagate this content in their social circles. Social networks provide easy means to distribute news and commentary, resulting in a sharp increase in the number of media outlets (Ribeiro et al., 2018), and a rapid spread of content. In particular, false news stories tend to spread at lightning speeds, and due to the volume, cannot be checked manually. An alternative to fact-checking claims, which is arguably easier to scale, is to focus on their source, and ask *who can you trust?*

Prior works have formulated this as a traditional classification problem using techniques such as feature-based SVM's (Baly et al., 2018, 2020), and more recently Graph Neural Networks (GNNs) (Li and Goldwasser, 2019; Shu et al., 2019; Han et al., 2020; Nguyen et al., 2020), which create a better representation of social media interactions. Graphs often consist of nodes corresponding to news sources (associated with a discrete factuality level - *high, low*, or *mixed*), the articles they release, and their social context, corresponding to social media users engaging and sharing information in their networks. GNNs can utilize this information by using edge interactions to create node representations contextualized by their graph neighbours. This leads to a stronger representation of the complex information landscape on social media that enables fake news to spread, allowing it to be better detected. For this reason, we adopt graphs as our automated framework (1).

Despite the success of these works, fake news detection is still a challenging research problem and human performance is significantly higher than fully automated systems (Shaar et al., 2020). Clearly, having humans fact check every information source is not scalable. Thus, our goal in this paper is to explore a different form of interaction with humans, where they can provide *advice* (Mehta and Goldwasser, 2019) to the automated system. Advice corresponds to localized judgements (provided through natural language) that help characterize the content and social interactions associated with sources. These judgements, associated with article and social media user nodes, are then propagated through the information graph using the GNN, allowing the system to take advantage of it to improve it's representation. As advice is not providing source labels directly, which is a time-consuming process requiring a global view of the source's interactions, it is scalable.

For example, one challenging aspect of the problem is that low-factuality ("fake news") sources may not always propagate false information (some of the articles they publish may be factual), and

Proceedings of the First Workshop on Interactive Learning for Natural Language Processing , pages 46–53
August 5, 2021. ©2021 Association for Computational Linguistics

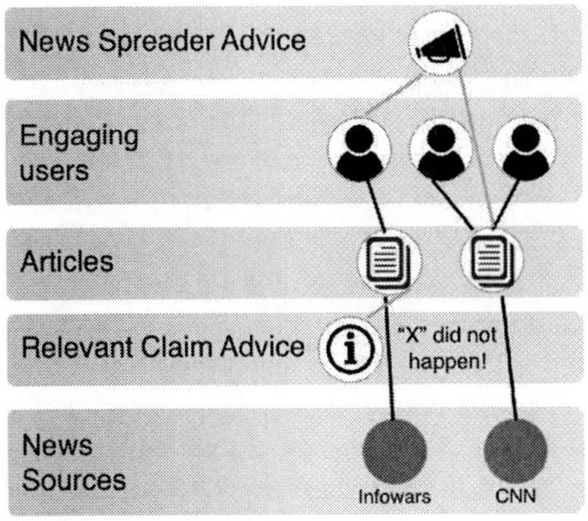

Figure 1: Information Graph capturing interactions between news sources, articles, and engaging users. Advice is added to the information graph by adding new nodes/edges(teal) based on the advice type (news spreader or relevant claims). Advice then provides information that can useful to clear up the complex social space the graph is modeling.

vice-versa (leading to model confusion). Human interaction, in the form of advice, can help clean up some of this uncertainty, by identifying claims containing egregious falsehoods. The model could then use this information and trust sources making these claims less. We refer to this form of advice, mapping a specific article to known falsehoods as *relevant claim advice*. In another case, referred to as *news spreader advice*, a human could inform the system that a user that is spreading a sources' articles frequently spreads lies, which would increase the likelihood that that source and any other source this user spreads articles from are fake. Fig 1 shows how both of these advice types can be seamlessly added to an information graph.

In this work, we show that our protocol in which humans iteratively provide these types of advice by interacting with the model (even after it is trained) improves overall fake news detection performance. In summary, we formulate fake news source detection as a reasoning problem over an information graph. We then suggest an interactive learning based approach for incorporating human knowledge as *advice* to clean up uncertain graph decisions, which allows us to better learn and reason on this graph. Finally, we perform experiments that demonstrate that this setup leads to performance improvements on fake news source detection.

2 Model

2.1 Graph Creation and Training

We start with defining our social context information graph. It consists of sources (S), articles they publish (A), and Twitter users that interact with sources/articles (U). Our goal is fake news source factuality classification. Each node in the graph is represented by a high dimensional feature vector, (similar to prior work (Baly et al., 2018, 2020; Nguyen et al., 2020)) to provide knowledge to the model that can be utilized when learning the graph embedding. Source and user feature vectors are created by concatenating embeddings based on their Twitter profiles (SBERT + features, details in Appendix A.2.1). Sources also can include YouTube profile embeddings. Articles are represented by the encoding text into a SBERT RoBERTa embedding.

Our graph is formed by first adding all the sources as individual nodes. We then scrape and add up to 300 articles (a_i) for each source, connecting each with an edge to the source that published it ($e = \{s_i, a_j\}$). Next, we add social context to the graph via Twitter users that interact with sources. We add up to 5000 users that follow sources, and users that tweet links to any articles in the graph within a 3 month period of the article being published ($e = \{s_i, u_j\}$, $e = \{a_i, u_j\}$). Users that follow/engage with sources are likely to be aligned with/propagating the view of the sources, and modeling this can be useful. Finally, in order to capture the social interactions between users in the graph, which is critical to capturing fake news propagation on social media, we scrape up to 5000 followers of each Twitter user and make an edge between a pair of existing users if one user follows another.

In order to learn the information captured by our information graph, we train a GNN to learn an initial embedding, on top of which we will apply the interactive protocols (Sec 2.2). As a node embedding function, we utilize Relational Graph Convolutional Networks (R-GCN) (Schlichtkrull et al., 2018) (they can handle the social media relationships well). We achieve meaningful representations and capture factuality of the different nodes in our graph by optimizing the Node Classification (NC) objective of Fake News Detection. After obtaining the source representations o_s from the R-GCN, we pass them through the softmax activation function σ and then train using categorical cross-entropy loss: $L_{nc} = -\sum_{i=1}^{C} y_i log(\sigma(o_s))$ where the C classes for y_i are either *high*, *mixed*, or *low* factuality, and s is the current source.

2.2 Advice Protocols

We now describe the two advice protocols we utilize in this paper. As mentioned in the introduction, in this work, we define advice as a form of human provided judgement (typically provided through natural language) about intermediate relationships in the information graph, that cleans up the space of complex judgements made by the GNN, allowing us to better capture the challenging landscape on social media that enables fake news to spread (Fig 1). Advice is provided by humans interactively and continuously, so that the process is scalable (not many judgements are needed, and they can always be provided, even after the system is deployed). In this way, our advice protocols provide a mechanism for humans to interact with the automated graph system. We use two forms of advice:

2.2.1 Relevant Claim Advice

When a human provides relevant claim advice, they have some prior knowledge about a certain claim (or news statement), and are telling this information (the claim and what their belief about its' factuality is) to the model . For example, a human may know that a certain claim is not factual (perhaps many users on social media spread it and thus the human has seen it before). The human would then provide this claim and a message about its factuality through natural language.

Once a human has provided advice in the form of a claim that may be relevant, the model must decide which articles (if any) the claim is relevant for. Once it does so, it can add a *new node* in the graph for the claim (represented similar to the article text node with SBERT RoBERTa embedding), and connect it to the relevant article(s), allowing the advice knowledge to easily propagate through the graph (either by re-training the GNN or using the trained GNN to embed the advice node appropiately $\rightarrow$ we evaluate both setups in Sec 3). This automated setup allows for minimal effort needed from the human, making the advice simple to provide.

To do this, first, the model filters a subset of sources (a process which we call *filtering*), whose articles could be candidates to receive advice. As mentioned earlier, advice cleans up complexities in the information graph, so these sources are ones which the model predicts the label of with low confidence (we rank Softmax scores for this). Then, for each filtered source's article, the model decides if the claim provided by the human is relevant, by analyzing content in two ways. **(1)** First, a heuristic is used to determine if the advice and article are talking about the same event. To do this, the model extracts the entities from the advice claim and the article (we use the FLAIR tagger (Akbik et al., 2019)), and determines if any of them overlap. If they do, the model also checks the date the advice claim was made, and makes sure it is within a one week period of the article being published. **(2)** Then, to further check content relevance, we use an entailment model (Parikh et al., 2016) and a sentence selection model (Nie et al., 2019) to check if any sentences from the article (chosen by the sentence selection model) entail the advice claim. If they do, the chance that the two are talking about similar content is higher. If there is an entailment, the advice statement d node is connected to the article a with an edge. All advice is also connected to a special label node h, m, or l, representing 'high', 'low', or 'mixed' factuality, based on the advice label (which is provided by the human), so that the model can easily represent that information.

In our interactive process, which we evaluate in Sec 3.2, a human can continuously provide relevant claims (through natural language) based on knowledge they posses as advice, and through the process described above, the model can determine which articles to use it for (thus connecting the advice in the graph). In this way, the human interacts with the system to clear up potential confusion about certain articles, which propagates via the graph through sources and users, to lead to better fake news detection performance.

2.2.2 News Spreader Advice

When providing news spreader advice, the human informs the system that a certain user is a *bad actor*, meaning that they frequently spread lies. This knowledge would increase the likelihood that articles this user tweets, and other users they interact with, are also non-factual. The user is then connected via an edge to a special 'low' factuality node, signifying to the model the set of users that are deemed to not be trusted.

2.2.3 Simulating Advice

In this preliminary work, we simulate the two previous forms of human provided advice by collecting data from fact-checking websites (PolitiFact, Snopes, USA Today, The Washington Post) and Twitter (details in Appendix A.1). For relevant

Model	Performance		
	Acc	Macro F1	# of Advice
M1 : Majority class	52.43	22.93	-
M2 : Best Model from (Baly et al., 2020)	71.52	**67.25**	-
M3 : Our replication of (Baly et al., 2020)	69.38	63.63	-
M4 : Node classification (NC)	65.76	55.97	-
M5 : Relevant Claim All Advice	69.02	61.89	29,673
M6 : Relevant Claim Advice Filtering 25%	68.09	60.28	17,305
M7 : Relevant Claim Advice Selection	70.54	62.61	4,106
M8 : Relevant Claim Advice Filtering + Selection 50% + 50%	68.56	60.80	4,106
M9 : Relevant Claim All Advice Match Label	76.36	70.89	8,677
M10 : News Spreader Only Bad	67.40	59.57	2,643
M11 : News Spreader Bad 50%	65.91	58.65	1,350
M12 : News Spreader Bad 50% + 50%	66.35	58.26	2,643

Table 1: Final results.

claim advice, we scrape all claims fact-checked by these websites and their factuality scores, and use that. This simulates humans providing advice in the real world, as a claim and some factuality insight about it are given. For news spreader advice, we use the Twitter API to determine all users that have been suspended since we initially collected our dataset, and use them as our news spreaders. Twitter manually suspended most of these users after the storming of the US capitol, so using this data allows us to accurately simulate human advice.

Although in this work we did not explicitly ask users to provide advice based on our learned graph model, our approximation of human advice that we collected was provided by human experts, and is thus relatively close to real advice that a human could provide. Relevant claims advice is based on real news claims that experts have associated factuality labels with, and Twitter manually suspended the users we used for news spreader advice.

3 Experiments

3.1 Dataset and Collection

To evaluate our model's ability to predict the factuality of news medium, we used the Media Bias/Fact Check (MBFC) dataset (Baly et al., 2018, 2020) (859 sources, each labeled on a 3-point scale based on their factuality: *low*, *mixed*, and *high*). We provide graph statistics in App. A.

3.2 Fake News Classification

Table 1 shows our results. We average our models on all 5 data splits released by (Baly et al., 2020), using 20% of the training set sources as a development set, and report results on accuracy and Macro F1-score for fake news source classification. We compare our advice protocol models to the baseline-graph based model trained only on node classification (NC - no advice provided, M4). For completeness, we included the results of the SOTA (Baly et al., 2020) (M2), as well as replication of their setup using the data we scraped (and their code). Our results are worse than their released performance, so we hypothesize that their data on our setup may lead to better overall performance.

For relevant claim advice, we evaluate settings in which we provide all the advice we scraped (29,673 statements - M5), where we provide advice only to the bottom 25% of sources that our model is not confident on during train/dev/test time (M6, all advice that passes the event filter is used → at least one entity in the articles title matches the advice claim and the dates are within one week of each other), and where we provide advice to all sources and make sure articles pass the event + entailment + sentence selection criteria (M7 - full setup in Sec 2.2.1). In all these setups, the advice is provided on the best model in M4, and then parameters are reset and the model is re-trained to learn how to incorporate the advice. M8 is different and more interactive, as advice is first provided on the bottom 50% of confident sources based on the protocol in Sec 2.2.1, then the model is re-trained. Then, the rest of the advice is provided as in M7, except this time the model isn't retrained. This simulates advice being continuously provided interactively by the human in the real world, and performance still improves. In this setting, as no re-training of the model is necessary, advice can be quickly utilized. All setups improve performance from the baseline, and using the filtering + sentence selection approach (M7) leads to the best performance, showing that the content of the advice matching the article matters. Thus, in the future when humans provide advice that is more likely to match the content of the articles, it is likely that we will see further performance improvements. Further, it is likely that less advice will need to be provided to see improvements.

For completeness, in M9 we also evaluate an upper bound, where advice provided by the human would be 100% accurate, i.e. the human would only provide advice that matched the article label (article label based on the label of the source).

Finally, we evaluate news spreader advice, first when all news spreaders are told to the model (M10), then when only 50% are (M11), and finally when 50% are told, the model is retrained, and then the rest are provided (M12, simulating true interaction).

In all advice models, performance improves from the NC baseline, showing that these types of advice can be helpful to the model. Furthermore, once the advice is provided, we can add more (M8, M12), and still see performance improvements without having to retrain the model, demonstrating a true interactive scenario, where a human can continuously be interacting with an automated system. In addition, providing advice as a localized judgement is simple and easier than labelling an entire source, so large amounts of advice can be collected from different experts to improve results. In the future, when we experiment with humans providing advice that is more content relevant (not simulating), the amount of advice needed could also decrease.

3.3 How Does Advice Help?

In this section, we analyze a few specific cases of how relevant claim advice is used by the model to improve performance. In one case, an article from a news source labeled as spreading fake news was discussing how a Democratic leader would become Vice President if the President was impeached. Our model incorrectly predicted the factuality of this source. However, an advice claim from Snopes stating that the 25th amendment would not lead to this Democratic candidate immediately becoming Vice President was able to push the prediction of the source in the appropriate direction. In another case, advice that a specific former President was the first to speak against the current President was provided through PolitiFact with a False label, pushing a different source towards the fake news label.

4 Summary and Future Work

In this paper, we proposed an approach to tackle fake news detection interactively by designing a protocol for a graph based system to continuously solicit human advice, and take advantage of it to improve overall information quality, which enables better fake news detection performance. We showed the benefits of two forms of advice (relevant claims and news spreaders), provided either all at once or continuously. In the future, we plan to have humans actually provide this advice, and explore other advice types.

5 Acknowledgments

We thank the anonymous reviewers of this paper for all of their vital feedback. This works was partially supported by an NSF CAREER award IIS-2048001. Any opinions, findings and conclusions or recommendations expressed in this material are those of the author(s) and do not necessarily reflect the views of the NSF.

6 Ethics Statement

To the best of our knowledge no code of ethics was violated throughout the experiments done in this paper. We reported all hyper-parameters and other technical details necessary to reproduce our results. For space constraint we moved some of the technical details to the Appendix section which is submitted with this manuscript. The results we reported supports our claims in this paper and we believe it is reproducible. Any qualitative result we report is an outcome from a machine learning model that does not represent the authors' personal views. Any results that we discussed on the data we used did not include account information and all results are anonymous. We anonymized the Twitter, article, and advice (Politifact, Snopes, USA Today, The Washington Post) data we collected to respect the privacy policy of the various websites and user data. While our overall approach does rely on user insights, each advice statement provided does not directly affect the final prediction, so a system receiving advice for fake news detection can not be easily manipulated.

References

Alan Akbik, Tanja Bergmann, Duncan Blythe, Kashif Rasul, Stefan Schweter, and Roland Vollgraf. 2019. Flair: An easy-to-use framework for state-of-the-art nlp. In *NAACL 2019, 2019 Annual Conference of the North American Chapter of the Association for Computational Linguistics (Demonstrations)*, pages 54–59.

Michael Barthel Elisa Shearer Amy Mitchell, Jeffrey Gottfried. 2016. The modern news consumer. *Pew Research Center*.

Ramy Baly, Georgi Karadzhov, Dimitar Alexandrov, James Glass, and Preslav Nakov. 2018. Predicting factuality of reporting and bias of news media sources. In *Proceedings of the Conference on Empirical Methods in Natural Language Processing*, EMNLP '18, Brussels, Belgium.

Ramy Baly, Georgi Karadzhov, Jisun An, Haewoon Kwak, Yoan Dinkov, Ahmed Ali, James Glass, and Preslav Nakov. 2020. What was written vs. who read it: News media profiling using text analysis and social media context. In *Proceedings of the 58th Annual Meeting of the Association for Computational Linguistics*, ACL '20.

Felix Hamborg, Norman Meuschke, Corinna Breitinger, and Bela Gipp. 2017. news-please: A generic news crawler and extractor. In *Proceedings of the 15th International Symposium of Information Science*, pages 218–223.

Yi Han, Shanika Karunasekera, and Christopher Leckie. 2020. Graph neural networks with continual learning for fake news detection from social media. *arXiv preprint arXiv:2007.03316*.

Chang Li and Dan Goldwasser. 2019. Encoding social information with graph convolutional networks forpolitical perspective detection in news media. In *Proceedings of the 57th Annual Meeting of the Association for Computational Linguistics*, pages 2594–2604.

Yinhan Liu, Myle Ott, Naman Goyal, Jingfei Du, Mandar Joshi, Danqi Chen, Omer Levy, Mike Lewis, Luke Zettlemoyer, and Veselin Stoyanov. 2019. Roberta: A robustly optimized bert pretraining approach. *arXiv preprint arXiv:1907.11692*.

Nikhil Mehta and Dan Goldwasser. 2019. Improving natural language interaction with robots using advice. In *Proceedings of the 2019 Conference of the North American Chapter of the Association for Computational Linguistics: Human Language Technologies, Volume 1 (Long and Short Papers)*, pages 1962–1967.

Van-Hoang Nguyen, Kazunari Sugiyama, Preslav Nakov, and Min-Yen Kan. 2020. Fang: Leveraging social context for fake news detection using graph representation. In *Proceedings of the 29th ACM International Conference on Information & Knowledge Management*, pages 1165–1174.

Yixin Nie, Haonan Chen, and Mohit Bansal. 2019. Combining fact extraction and verification with neural semantic matching networks. In *Proceedings of the AAAI Conference on Artificial Intelligence*, volume 33, pages 6859–6866.

Ankur P Parikh, Oscar Täckström, Dipanjan Das, and Jakob Uszkoreit. 2016. A decomposable attention model for natural language inference. *arXiv preprint arXiv:1606.01933*.

Adam Paszke, Sam Gross, Francisco Massa, Adam Lerer, James Bradbury, Gregory Chanan, Trevor Killeen, Zeming Lin, Natalia Gimelshein, Luca Antiga, Alban Desmaison, Andreas Kopf, Edward Yang, Zachary DeVito, Martin Raison, Alykhan Tejani, Sasank Chilamkurthy, Benoit Steiner, Lu Fang, Junjie Bai, and Soumith Chintala. 2019. Pytorch: An imperative style, high-performance deep learning library. In H. Wallach, H. Larochelle, A. Beygelzimer, F. d'Alché-Buc, E. Fox, and R. Garnett, editors, *Advances in Neural Information Processing Systems 32*, pages 8024–8035. Curran Associates, Inc.

Nils Reimers and Iryna Gurevych. 2019. Sentence-bert: Sentence embeddings using siamese bert-networks. *arXiv preprint arXiv:1908.10084*.

Filipe N Ribeiro, Lucas Henrique, Fabricio Benevenuto, Abhijnan Chakraborty, Juhi Kulshrestha, Mahmoudreza Babaei, and Krishna P Gummadi. 2018. Media bias monitor: Quantifying biases of social media news outlets at large-scale. In *Twelfth International AAAI Conference on Web and Social Media*.

Michael Schlichtkrull, Thomas N Kipf, Peter Bloem, Rianne Van Den Berg, Ivan Titov, and Max Welling. 2018. Modeling relational data with graph convolutional networks. In *European semantic web conference*, pages 593–607. Springer.

Shaden Shaar, Alex Nikolov, Nikolay Babulkov, Firoj Alam, Alberto Barrón-Cedeno, Tamer Elsayed, Maram Hasanain, Reem Suwaileh, Fatima Haouari, Giovanni Da San Martino, et al. 2020. Overview of checkthat! 2020 english: Automatic identification and verification of claims in social media. *Cappellato et al.[10]*.

Kai Shu, Suhang Wang, and Huan Liu. 2019. Beyond news contents: The role of social context for fake news detection. In *Proceedings of the twelfth ACM international conference on web search and data mining*, pages 312–320.

Minjie Wang, Da Zheng, Zihao Ye, Quan Gan, Mufei Li, Xiang Song, Jinjing Zhou, Chao Ma, Lingfan Yu, Yu Gai, et al. 2019. Deep graph library: A graph-centric, highly-performant package for graph neural networks. *arXiv preprint arXiv:1909.01315*.

A Supplemental Material

In this section, we provide implementation details for our models. The dataset we use has 859 sources: 452 *high* factuality, 245 *mixed*, and 162 *low*, and was released publicly by (Baly et al., 2020)[1]. The dataset does not include any other raw data (articles, sources, etc.), so we must scrape our own.

A.1 Data Collection

For each source, we attempted to scrape news articles using public libraries (Newspaper3K [2], Scrapy [3], and news-please [4] (Hamborg et al., 2017)). In the cases where the web pages of the source news articles was removed, we used the Wayback Machine [5]. Overall, our sources have an average of 109 articles with a STD of 36.

For Twitter users, we used the Twitter API[6] to scrape 5000 followers for each Twitter account we could find (72.5% of the sources, identical to (Baly et al., 2020). In the graph, we then connected these users to the sources they follow. In addition, we used the Twitter Search API to search articles on Twitter and find any Tweets that mention the article title or URL within 3 months of the article being published. We then downloaded the users that make these Tweets as well, and added them to our graph, linking them to the respective article they talk about. Finally, to increase the connectivity of the graph and accurately capture the interactions between the users, we also scraped the followers of every Twitter user. We then made sure to only add users to our graph that either interact with multiple sources (through source or article connections) or another user, so that every node would be interconnected.

We did not scrape YouTube accounts, but rather used the same ones as the ones released by (Baly et al., 2020). They found YouTube channels for 49% of sources.

For collecting relevant claim advice from news sources (PolitiFact, Snopes, USA Today, and the Washington Post), we used the Google FactCheck tool[7], along with scraping the PolitiFact website. We downloaded 29,673 claims in total.

[1] https://github.com/ramybaly/News-Media-Reliability

[2] https://github.com/codelucas/newspaper

[3] https://github.com/scrapy/scrapy

[4] https://github.com/fhamborg/news-please

[5] https://archive.org/web/

[6] https://developer.twitter.com/en/docs

[7] https://toolbox.google.com/factcheck/explorer

A.2 Experimental Settings

A.2.1 Initial Embeddings

Our initial Twitter embedding for each source and engaging user was a 773 dimensional vector consisting the SBERT (Reimers and Gurevych, 2019) (RoBERTa (Liu et al., 2019) Base NLI model) representation of their bio concatenated with the following numerical features: a binary number representing whether the source is verified, the number users a source follows and the number that follow it, the number of tweets it makes, and the number of favorites/likes its' tweets have received. For, YouTube, the embedding we used was the average of the number of views, dislikes, and comments for each video the source posted. Sources that did not have a YouTube channel had a random YouTube embedding. For articles, we used the SBERT (Reimers and Gurevych, 2019) RoBERTa (Liu et al., 2019) model to generate an embedding for each article. For relevant claims advice, we used the same SBERT (Reimers and Gurevych, 2019) RoBERTa (Liu et al., 2019) model to generate an embedding for each advice claim.

We also mentioned special factuality nodes in Sec 2.2.1 that are added into the graph and connected to advice claims, to allow the model to easily represent the advice label (either the claim label or the fact that a Twitter user is spreading bad news). These nodes are initialized randomly with a 768 dimensional embedding that is then learned when the graph is re-trained after the initial set of advice is added.

A.3 Graph Statistics

We downloaded an average of 109 articles per source, with a STD of 36, and user-engagements (talking about articles, following sources/other users) via the Twitter API [8](sources have an average of 27 users directly connected to them or to their articles). Using this data we construct the graph as described in Sec 2.1, which consists of 69,978 users, 93,191 articles, 164,034 nodes, and 7,196,808 edges. Details about the model setup we utilized when training our graph (chosen using the development set), and our scraping protocol are in Appendix A.

A.3.1 Model Setup

Our models are built on top of PyTorch (Paszke et al., 2019) and DGL (Deep Graph Library) (Wang

[8] https://developer.twitter.com/en/docs

et al., 2019) in Python. The R-GCN we use consists of 5 layers, 128 hidden units, a learning rate of 0.001, and a batch size of 128 for Node Classification. Our initial source, article, and advice embeddings have hidden dimension 768, while the user one has dimension 773.

We choose parameters using the development set (20% of train sources) for one of the training data splits, and then apply them uniformly across all the splits, when training the final models. We choose the stopping point for the best performing models on which to apply advice on top of based on the dev set. In the setups where we did not apply all the advice at once, we determined all the advice that could be relevant and then randomly chosen which ones to apply based on the percentage of the total the experiment required.

Our models were trained on a 12GB TITAN XP GPU card and training each data split for Node Classification takes approximately 4 hours, while training Link Prediction Pre-training and the combined initialization step takes 24 hours.

A.3.2 Replication of Prior Work

To replicate (Baly et al., 2020) (`M3`), we used their released code with our features. Specifically, we used our article, Twitter profile, Twitter Follower, and YouTube embeddings. This setup consists of all the data in our graph, and also provided the best performance in (Baly et al., 2020).

Author Index

Association for Computational Linguistics
209 N. Eighth Street
Stroudsburg, Pennsylvania 18360

CURRAN ASSOCIATES INC.
proceedings
.com

ISBN 978-1-7138-3376-5
9 781713 833765